LACANIAN
PSYCHOTHERAPY

LACANIAN PSYCHOTHERAPY

Theory and Practical Applications

Michael J. Miller

Routledge
Taylor & Francis Group
New York London

Routledge
Taylor & Francis Group
711 Third Avenue
New York, NY 10017

Routledge
Taylor & Francis Group
2 Park Square, Milton Park
Abingdon, Oxon OX14 4RN

International Standard Book Number: 978-0-415-89304-6 (Hardback) 978-0-415-89305-3 (Paperback)

Library of Congress Cataloging-in-Publication Data

Miller, Michael J. (Michael Joseph), 1976- author.
Lacanian psychotherapy : theory and practical applications / Michael J. Miller.
p. ; cm.
Includes bibliographical references and index.
ISBN 978-0-415-89304-6 (hardcover : alk. paper) -- ISBN 978-0-415-89305-3 (softcover : alk. paper) -- ISBN 978-0-203-81709-4 (e-book)
1. Psychoanalysis. 2. Lacan, Jacques, 1901-1981. I. Title.
[DNLM: 1. Lacan, Jacques, 1901-1981. 2. Psychoanalytic Theory. 3. Psychoanalytic Therapy--methods. WM 460]

RC506.M525 2011
616.89'17--dc22

2010047978

Visit the Taylor & Francis Web site at
http://www.taylorandfrancis.com

and the Routledge Web site at
http://www.routledgementalhealth.com

Dedicated to my grandmother, Jean, with gratitude
for all she has taught me about love and healing.

Lucky us.

Contents

Acknowledgments

This book exists primarily because of the trust, hard work, and awe-inspiring resilience and inner health of the patients I have written about here. I also owe a huge debt to the support, direct and indirect, of many great friends and colleagues. Chief among them is Dr. Bruce Fink, who introduced me to clinical and serious theoretical thinking about Lacan, and who has kindly tolerated the way I have twisted his lessons into what you are about to read. He contributed close reading and thoughtful critique during the early stages of the manuscript. My great thanks go also to Routledge, and especially Kristopher Spring, for taking a chance on this publication. I am also grateful for the support and helpful comments and suggestions of Drs. Paul Richer and Russell Walsh of Duquesne University. Dr. Jamie Ghany read this manuscript in its entirety several times over, somehow retained her good will toward me, and provided extremely valuable feedback. Dr. Sipho Mbuqe and Rong-Bang Peng provided support, commentary, and thoughtful discussion of all things psychoanalytic, philosophical, and beyond throughout the writing process.

About the Patients

All identifying information has been removed from or heavily disguised in the following case studies, so that no reader (except, possibly, the patient her- or himself) will be able to identify who is being discussed. The symbolic relationships between aspects of these patients' stories, however, have been preserved.

Introduction: AnOther Psychoanalysis

> Man thus speaks, but it is because the symbol has made him man.
>
> —**Lacan (1953, p. 65)**

LACAN'S ABSENCE FROM THE AMERICAN CLINIC

Nearly a century after Freud (1918) first took up the question of the "narcissism of minor differences," the culture of psychoanalysis seems to have taken that art to new heights. An extraordinary appetite for factionalism, even as psychoanalysis in general languishes at the margins of American psychology, continues to splinter its adherents into innumerable camps. Indeed, it seems as though there may be as many types of psychoanalysis as there are theoreticians and practitioners. But this is not entirely a bad thing. This tradition imparts to the student of psychoanalysis an embarrassment of theoretical riches, the opportunity to listen closely to any of the numerous voices from the dissonant chorus, and the challenge to test them philosophically in ways that often transcend simple questions of treatment efficacy.

Some voices are, of course, louder than others. In the United States, the legacy of ego psychology still looms large, while the relational turn dominates much of current discourse. And one arguably important voice is barely audible above the others.

A student of psychodynamic therapy in this country is hard-pressed to find a legitimate clinical education that involves any academic or practical work based on Jacques Lacan's contributions to psychoanalysis. Her exposure to Lacan is much more likely to come in the form of what she overhears in departments of literature and philosophy than it is to come from her psychological training. If the clinician in training wishes to take up Lacan clinically, she is largely on her own, even in psychoanalytic training institutes, faced with a shortage of mentorship, clinical literature, and camaraderie of like-minded professionals.

This is ostensibly not without reason. In the first place, Lacan's writing is often thought of as too bizarre and opaque to be rewarding to the reading clinician. This criticism is not entirely baseless: Lacan's prose is arguably on a par with James Joyce's in its level of obscurantism. But when challenged on these grounds, Lacan (1975/1998, p. 26) himself responded by declaring that his writing was never meant to be read, least of all by "idiots" (Lacan & Copjee, p. xxv). Such narcissistic rhetoric does little to ingratiate Lacan to readers who may be put off by his style. Yet for the challenge he represents to the reader, does Lacan deserve to be left aside by American psychotherapy, or is there something more that he has to offer us? To look at the more enthusiastic response his work has garnered in other parts of the world, one cannot but suspect that there is.

However obscure Lacan's writing may be, and however far from the American psychoanalytic (and therefore psychodynamic) mainstream it may remain, it should give us pause to realize his effect in other places, both geographic and academic. Curiously, as his analysand Stuart Schneiderman (1983) put it, Lacan "made a very successful career out of saying things that just about no one could understand" (p. vi). One measure of that success might be found in the fact that 4 years after his death in 1981, 19 of the 20 existing psychoanalytic organizations in France were basing their work on the teachings of Jacques Lacan (Nobus, 2000, p. 213). Along the way, he enlisted intellectuals of all stripes—philosophers, anthropologists, and most importantly for our purposes, *clinicians*—in an important rebellion against the psychoanalytic status quo of his time.

The nature of that rebellion, which I will discuss in the pages that follow, may have just as much to do with Lacan's lack of popularity in the United States as does his convoluted prose. Lacan's work was anything but kind to the strain of psychoanalysis made popular here under the auspices of Hartmann, Kris, and Loewenstein, among others (see Fink, 2004). Hence, the experience of the American analyst or analytic therapist who reads Lacan is made doubly unpleasant: Why spend time and effort reading work that insults not only the reader, but his ideological forbears as well, and does so in a way that is barely intelligible?

Despite all this, as a psychologist who has had the opportunity to gain some exposure to the clinical application of Lacan through academic work and clinical supervision, his conspicuous absence from the clinical scene in America strikes me as unfortunate. I have been experimenting for some time now in my own clinical work with applying Lacan, and feel that he has something unique and useful to offer the clinician. But the discursive (and cultural) gap between "Lacanians" and the rest of psychodynamic clinicians—never mind psychologists or psychotherapists in general—is often so great that it becomes difficult to communicate about ideas.

Perhaps this need not be the case. Malone and Friedlander (2000) have called for a "cross cultural dialogue" between American psychology and psychoanalysis via Lacan, and a similar dialogue between Lacanian theory and more mainstream American psychodynamic therapists may also be called for. Malone and Friedlander have, indeed, with a few others, begun to lay the groundwork for such a dialogue.

Even as authors such as Malone and Friedlander (2000), Nobus (2000), Schneiderman (1980, 1983), and Dor (1997a, 1997b) have begun the task of creating a body of literature wherein one serious clinician can hear from another about a viable approach to doing psychotherapy, their work with Lacanian theory tends to remain just that—theoretical. These authors leave us to wonder: What might a Lacanian approach to psychotherapy actually look like? What happens when we *use* Lacan? As with other clinical theories, one of the most rewarding ways to evaluate Lacan's may be through the chronicling of its attempted application.

Yet there are few concrete clinical illustrations of Lacan's theories, written such that they may be taken up constructively by the reader and considered as an option for practice. Lacan himself generally preferred to comment or critique cases already published; he did discuss one of his own cases in "The Direction of the Treatment and the Principles of its Power" (1961/2002), but the presentation was hardly comprehensive. Similarly, a number of Lacanian authors have turned to the analysis of existent texts or theoretical elaborations rather than the publication of their own clinical case material. While this gap in the literature is widely acknowledged—even lamented—few authors seem to try to remedy it. Jean-Michel Rabate makes this observation in his introduction to *Lacan in America* (2000), a volume that seeks to further a dialogue about Lacan in the North American context:

> [I]n a typically Lacanian manner, a number of clinical practitioners choose to address fundamental issues rather than make points based on case studies, as is regularly done in more traditional Freudian literature. The several Lacanian clinicians who write here [in North America] deliberately abstain from systematic discussions of clinical material, in keeping with Lacan's often-noted reluctance to engage in case discussions. (p. xxiv)

Oddly enough, not one of the essays that follow that introduction presents a case study.

Such is one problem in the literature that this book proposes to help address: the lack of concrete case discussions in a Lacanian framework.[1] I intend to take up what might be seen as Lacan's seminal objection to the stance of ego psychology—that it had lost sight of language as the proper domain of psychoanalysis. Through my own clinical case studies, I will attempt to illustrate the application of a Lacanian attitude toward listening to the patient's language "to the letter," and thereby the unique and fruitful ways in which it affects a course of psychotherapy.

My position as I take to this task is somewhat unique, as I am not a psychoanalyst, and therefore the cases I have written about were not analyses, although I do consider my work with these patients to have been analytic in nature. Rather, I conducted these therapies as a clinician who has had the good fortune to be exposed to a number of different ideas about doing psychotherapy, including various articulations of psychoanalysis, psychodynamic therapy, and existential and humanistic therapy. This admittedly curtails my rights to speak as an authority, and puts my project in danger of relying on too little knowledge. As Malone and Friedlander (2000) point out: "Much of the English-language psychological literature on Lacan is produced by authors who are not explicitly trained in 'Lacanian psychoanalysis.' Even when they themselves have positive impressions of Lacan, they may stumble on some of the more obscure turns in his thinking" (p. 3).

While this is a viable objection, I must clarify that my aim is not to speak as a psychoanalyst, nor do I wish to portray myself as an authority on all matters Lacanian. Rather, I am interested in

[1] A lack of case studies does not in itself suffice as a call for more case studies. After all, how many case studies will finally be enough? While this is obviously not an answerable question, it may be relevant to point out that at present, only one researcher (Goldman, 2004) has presented original case studies in American Lacanian psychotherapy (as opposed to psychoanalysis). Regardless of the question of what might constitute enough case studies, we might argue that a clinical approach must evolve via more than one voice, and that if Lacanian therapy is to become a viable field of study and practice, rather than an artifact, something akin to a dead language (which needs only one authoritative text to maintain itself as such), it must go beyond the form of monologue. Further, I argue below that the method of the case study stands on its own, regardless of the frequency or quantity of its representations, as a viable approach to answering the question of how one might apply a given theory, in this case Lacan's theory of the analysis of language.

telling the story of what happened when I applied some Lacanian principles to relatively short-term psychotherapies. This may be problematic to those who are invested in a purist approach to Lacanian praxis (whatever that may be), but I contend that my position—as a non-analyst—helps the honesty and rigor of this project. I can afford to be excited and fascinated by Lacan's work, hopefully without becoming its zealous missionary. As for the possibility that I will "stumble on some of the more obscure turns in [Lacan's] thinking," I am resigned to the possibility that I will stumble upon even the most basic, and I will leave it to the reader to agree or disagree with my interpretations.

A WORD ON THE WEIRD

Much of what follows will almost certainly strike the reader as counterintuitive, or maybe even a bit ridiculous. Let me say in advance that I am fully aware of that. There are a number of opportunities in these chapters to find the absurd, and to take issue with it, both of which I welcome and fully expect. While I am advocating a closer look at how Lacan can be useful, I am by no means a pious devotee of the methods I outline here. At the same time, what seems absurd in and of itself in fact only becomes absurd in a context. Our current psychotherapeutic *Zeitgeist* inherits from American pragmatism and scientific positivism a reverence for the face-valid and the apparently efficient, and even contemporary psychoanalysis has come to de-emphasize a Freudian unconscious in favor of a (perhaps less threatening) intuitionism. Part of what makes what is written here seem so strange is that this book, with Lacan, departs somewhat radically at times from those values.

What I have come to believe, and what I hope you'll consider as well, is that part of the unique value of psychoanalytic therapy lies precisely in its capacity to tolerate and foster the counterintuitive and the unconventional.

1

Shattering Discourse to Bring Forth Speech

> Whether it wishes to be an agent of healing, training, or sounding the depths, psychoanalysis has but one medium: the patient's speech.
>
> **—Lacan (1953/2002, p. 40)**

Jacques Lacan, a rising star on the psychoanalytic scene, although already a controversial figure for his variable-length session, found himself in January of 1953 the newly elected president of the *Société Psychanalytique de Paris* (SPP) (Nobus, 2000, p. 193). He was, via that institution and its affiliation with the International Psychoanalytic Association, invited to address the upcoming Annual Congress of Romance Language–Speaking Psychoanalysts in Rome on the subject of speech and language. "In the meantime," he tells us, "serious disagreements," largely over Lacan's use of the variable length session, "led to a secession within the French group" (1953/2002, p. 31).[1] Lacan in turn resigned his position at the SPP 6 months after attaining it to join those who had seceded in the newly formed *Société Française de Psychanalyse* (SFP).

Despite the mounting political tension surrounding Lacan, he was allowed to make the address he had been invited for, and the members of the SFP were allowed to attend. During that

[1] My references to essays contained in *Écrits* will correspond to Fink's pagination (Lacan, 2002, 2006).

address, nicknamed the "Rome Discourse," Lacan circulated a paper entitled "The Function and Field of Speech and Language in Psychoanalysis," a work that might be seen (or heard) as the "newborn's cry" (1953/2002, p. 32) of a Lacanian psychoanalysis. At the least, it provides the reader with one possible starting point from which to understand Lacan's agenda, which was at the core of the "serious disagreements" to which he alludes. That agenda was "to revamp the foundations our discipline derives from language" (p. 32).

With this paper, Lacan made plain what was at stake in his "return to Freud." His aim was to bring psychoanalysis back to what he saw as Freud's greatest discovery: simply put, that the "talking cure" was about *talking*.

Lacan also commented extensively on what, in his view, psychoanalysis was *not* about, and the tone of his critique leaves little doubt as to one aggravating factor in the rift between Lacan and his contemporaries. Unfortunately, this tone set the stage for a lasting schism between Lacan's vision of psychoanalysis and that of Kris, Loewenstein, Hartmann, Balint, and Winnicott, whose views (though hardly all one) have largely been constitutive of the impact made by psychoanalysis on current American psychodynamic therapy (see, for example, Jacobs, 1991; Maroda, 1999, 2001; McWilliams, 1994). Here we see a perennial problem with Lacan: In his attempts to move psychoanalytic praxis into the "symbolic" realm of productive dialogue, his politics and his rhetoric often leave us stuck in what Lacan (1988b) called "the imaginary," a narcissistic world of "us and them"; rivals who will not concede even to speak each other's names (Fink, 2004; Schneiderman, 1983).

THE "NEWBORN'S CRY" OF A LACANIAN PSYCHOANALYSIS

While any number of Lacan's texts will provide the reader with examples of what he found wrong with analysis as taken up by his contemporaries, it seems fitting to turn to the first cries of the newborn *enfant terrible* to orient ourselves. In "The Function and Field of Speech and Language in Psychoanalysis" (1953/2002), Lacan wastes little time in voicing what he sees as the problem:

> One can trace over the years a growing aversion regarding the functions of speech and the field of language. It is responsible for the "changes in aim and technique" that are acknowledged within the psychoanalytic movement, and whose relation to the general decline in therapeutic effectiveness is nevertheless ambiguous. (p. 34)

This "aversion regarding the functions of speech and the field of language" is to be found in an emphasis, in "the literature that we call our 'scientific activity,'" that is, a psychoanalysis as interpreted by ego psychologists and object-relations theorists, on "[t]he function of the imaginary … the concept of libidinal object relations … [and] the importance of countertransference" (pp. 242–243).

For Lacan, these new emphases in psychoanalysis constituted a shift away from the "symbolic" register—the proper domain of psychoanalysis, which involves a discourse between the "Subject" and the "Other"—and toward the "imaginary" register, by way of which two egos relate either in friendly identification ("me and somebody like me") or via adversarial posturing.

Psychoanalysis, as part of its acculturation to an American paradigm,[2] has become focused on *"communication" between egos as the curative factor in psychoanalytic treatment*. The analyst's ego communicates with, becomes a model for, and props up the ego of his analysand; that is, the psychoanalyst has been relegated simply to influencing the patient to be more like him.

"[P]sychoanalysis in the United States has been inflected toward the adaptation of the individual to the social environment, the

---

[2] Lacan (1953/2002) makes mention of the "convergence that occurs between the alien status of a group dominated by immigrants and the distance it is lured into taking from its roots by the function called for by … cultural conditions" (p. 39). Psychoanalysis, for Lacan, has become acculturated: an American immigrant who has forgotten her roots. Lacan's distaste for American culture is evident at several points in this essay, which again is not necessarily helpful to his cause here. As Gallop (1985) puts it, "The problem of translating or transferring the *Écrits* into the American scene is not simply to get the *Écrits* into American, but what to do about the America that is already in the *Écrits*" (p. 57).

search for behavior patterns, and all the objectification implied in the notion of 'human relations'" (p. 39). Rather than remain true to itself as an exploration of the symbolic and linguistic systems that structure the unconscious subject, as per his reading of Freud, psychoanalysis according to Lacan has become little more than a glorified exercise in behavior modification; a mirage of "communication," which leaves the subject without her own history (p. 39), has come to replace the proper analytic experience.

Further, Lacan argues that the analyst is mistaken in his notion that language and speech are fundamentally inadequate to the psychoanalytic project. As a result of this supposed mistake, the practice of analysis has become focused on an illusory something situated *beyond* speech, which makes itself known in an interpersonal, affective way.

Already, characterizing this focus of clinical practice as a mistake is bound to strike us as counterintuitive. To speak from my own experience as a student of psychodynamic therapy (which I imagine is not entirely unique), I have been trained to "follow the affect" of my patients and to pay constant attention to my countertransference feelings, and even to regard them as typical of the position that the client must tend to put others in. So interpersonal, relational experience as well as the importance of affect have been central to my own training, perhaps as a result of the influences Lacan was protesting. Yet some have gone further than the emphasis I have described and recommend that we actually *engage* these feelings in the session: to let the client know, for example, that I might be feeling angry "for"—or even *with*—him (see, for example, Jacobs, 1991; Maroda, 1999, 2001).

Intervention based at least partially on these interpersonal, intuitive aspects of our experience with the patient has sometimes been presented in psychodynamic training as preferable to acting on the basis of a prefabricated, intellectualized construction we may have reached. Indeed, some would maintain that to intervene based on the latter is often nothing short of colluding with the client, for we often see her as already too intellectually defended, and to make such a mistake would be to encourage her destructive interpersonal patterns via the defense with which I have allowed myself to become complicit, while what is really needed is for the client to be brought back to an authentic, interpersonal expression of an affective state that lies beyond words.[3]

Karen Maroda (2001) brings this idea to its logical (and perhaps chilling) conclusion when, discussing her disclosure of her anger with a client, she writes: "I realized how important the expression of my affect was to breaking through to Sally and patients like her. *Sadism was preferable to my neutrality*" (p. 34, emphasis added).

Not so, says Lacan (1953/2002), with some contempt of his own:

> [N]othing could be more misleading for the analyst than to seek to guide himself by some supposed "contact" he experiences with the subject's reality. This vacuous buzzword of intuitionist and even phenomenological psychology has become extended in contemporary usage in a way that is thoroughly symptomatic of the ever scarcer effects of speech in the present social context. But its obsessive value becomes flagrant when it is recommended in a relationship which, according to its very rules, excludes all real contact. (p. 39)

For Lacan, to entirely base an approach to treatment upon such interpersonal "contact," using as our guide our own countertransference fantasies, feelings, and intuitions, boils down to little more than an exercise in narcissism. To intervene based upon hunches about the patient's affect, and to privilege an affectively based "contact" beyond that of language, is to miss the point of Freud's "Promethean" discovery as illustrated in *The Psychopathology of*

[3] Curiously, though, work with language (the "one medium" of psychoanalysis, according to Lacan) has often been somehow equated with the defense of intellectualization: Too much focus on words takes away from a focus on wordless affect. This substitution of "language" for "intellect" seems a bit dubious, given that, on examination, affect is communicated and constituted largely by language. This is not to say that there is no preverbal component to affect, but rather to note that once affect has language to describe it, it is necessarily informed by that language. "Feeling blue" is arguably a different experience than *tristesse*, if only by means of the fact that each occurs within a different cultural context and brings different associations with it, which in turn give the affective experience its own specific timbre.

Everyday Life (1904), *Jokes and Their Relation to the Unconscious* (1905b), *The Interpretation of Dreams* (1900), "Notes Upon a Case of Obsessional Neurosis" (1909), and "Fragments of an Analysis of a Case of Hysteria" (1905a), to name a few—that the subject exists and is always to be found in language itself.

But what is at stake for Lacan is more than simply an appreciation of one of the philosophical underpinnings of Freud's work. Rather, "[b]ringing psychoanalytic experience back to speech and language as its foundations is of direct concern to its technique" (Lacan, 1953/2002, p. 76).

To better understand what it might mean for Lacan to be accusing his contemporaries of propagating a narcissistic psychoanalysis, we must return briefly to his conception of the ego, noting that he maintained that this concept of Freud's, too, was misappropriated by the ego psychologists. Lacan accuses ego psychology of *misconstruing* the ego as a "reality function" (although this is in fact reflective of Freud's later conceptions of it) and insinuates that his acculturated peers have been mistakenly seduced by the belief that "the subject's ego is identical to the presence that is speaking …" (p. 88).

For Lacan, nothing could be further from the truth. As we see first in "The Mirror Stage as Formative of the *I* Function" (1949/2002), Lacan sets up the ego as the *symptom* upon which he begins to construct the imaginary register. Briefly put, the ego for Lacan is the locus of mistaken identity: a *misrecognition* by the subject of itself as a two-dimensional image. Maintaining that he is in line with Freud on this question, he refers to the ego (1953/2002) as "the system of the subject's objectifications" (p. 88). The ego for Lacan is itself an objectification; the fundamental objectification, a primary symptom that sets the stage for ensuing symptoms over the course of a lifetime, which finally lead the patient to psychoanalysis. If this is the nature of the ego, then it must be counterproductive for the analyst to simply align herself with the patient's ego: This would be nothing other than strengthening the disease in hope of a cure.

This is precisely the direction in which Lacan sees psychoanalysis heading as it strays from its engagement in speech and language in favor of attending to affect, countertransference, intuition, and the like as they culminate in a curative relationship between analyst and patient. Michael Balint's (1968) notion of a "two-body psychology" is used as an example:

> Analysis is becoming the relation of two bodies between which a fantasmatic communication is established in which the analyst teaches the subject to apprehend himself as an object. Subjectivity is admitted into analysis only as long as it is bracketed as an illusion, and speech is excluded from a search for lived experience that becomes its supreme aim. (Lacan, 1953/2002, p. 304)

In the search for an intersubjective, two-body, perhaps emotionally corrective relationship, analysis succeeds only in *objectifying* the patient, giving her an even stronger (read: more restrictive) ego than the one that led her to the analyst in the first place, and imprisoning her subjectivity even more radically than it had been before. Worse yet, the analyst can only give the patient one kind of new ego: one that is modeled on the analyst's own. As Lacan puts it, we risk the subject's "being captured in an objectification—no less imaginary than before—of his stationary state, indeed, of his statue, in a renewed status of his alienation" (p. 43). For Lacan, then, when that statue is to be sculpted by the hands of the analyst for whom the patient has become a mirror of sorts, analysis has become a narcissistic project. Gallop (1985) puts it succinctly: "The enterprise of ego psychology reshapes the analysand's imagoes into ones that better correspond to 'reality'—that is, to the analyst's reality. ... The analysand ... has simply substituted the analyst's imaginary for his own" (p. 61).

FOLLOWING THE LETTER: THE ANALYSIS OF LANGUAGE

Lacan proposes that this impasse, brought about along the imaginary axis between two egos, is to be avoided by attending to the symbolic axis: the register of speech and language. This is not to be taken as a purely intellectual exercise, and not therefore as collusive with a patient's intellectual defenses. Indeed, why equate language with intellectual defenses at all? Rather, we find in the end that speech and language are the best indicators we have of a patient's *subjectivity*, and that if we are to meet the subject at all, it must be by the road of his speech rather than that of our imaginary identifications: "The analyst's art must … involve suspending the subject's certainties until their final mirages have been consumed. And it is in the subject's discourse that their dissolution must be punctuated" (p. 251).

But this requires the analyst to listen, to take up the patient's speech, in a way that is different from what we are used to, or intuitively comfortable with. The analyst is not to listen for what the patient *means*: "*I* know what *you* mean" is the alignment of speech with the imaginary register, and thereby with the ego, which is the problem in the first place. It tells the subject that his speech is unimportant and that what matters is that the analyst's ego is identified with the patient's: "I understand you. I am like you. You are like me."

Instead, we might say that the analyst is not to take the patient at her word. Better put, he is not to invest in *her* word, the word spoken in service of the ego's intentions. Rather, he is to take the patient at her *word*. Hence an exchange between analyst and patient like the following:

P: And when I get home, I'd like to relax, sit down in front of the TV and turn er on—turn it on.
A: Turn er on?
P: I meant to say "turn it on." You know what I mean.
A: Hm. You said "turn er on."

This attention to the letter, rather than the "spirit" or intention of the patient's speech, lies at the heart of Lacan's "return to Freud." Lacan maintains what he sees as fidelity to Freud by regarding symptoms, fantasies, and dreams (and of course, the speech of the patient) as conforming to the structure of language. And language does not operate via a singular relationship between signified and signifier (Saussure, 1986; Lacan, 1957/2002, 1988a), but is characterized by a complex interrelationship via metaphor and metonymy between one signifier and others. Using this Freudian/Saussurian conception of language, Lacan (1953/2002) redefines psychoanalytic anamnesis not as a means of finding out some ultimate objective reality (p. 47), but as a symbolic matter of discovering truth via a re-understanding (or re-membering) of the text of the patient's speech in its various forms.

> The unconscious is the chapter of my history that is marked by a blank or occupied by a lie: It is the censored chapter. But the truth can be refound, most often it has already been written elsewhere. Namely, in … the hysterical symptom [that] manifests the structure of a language, and is deciphered like an inscription which, once recovered, can be destroyed without serious loss; in archival documents, too: These are my childhood memories; in semantic evolution: this corresponds to the stock of words and acceptations of my own particular vocabulary, as it does to my style of life and my character; in traditions, too, and even in the legends which … convey my history. (p. 50)

Symptoms, memories, dreams, and speech itself, then, are to be regarded in psychoanalysis as all conforming to the structure of language, and the attention of the analyst must privilege their symbolic (or linguistic) nature over and above the kind of interpersonal, egoic contact discussed above.

But the kind of privileged attention given to this register by the analyst is also at issue. Lacan is not advising the analyst to correct grammatical mistakes, for example, or to help the subject improve his public speaking skills. Rather, with Freud, Lacan recognizes the overdetermination and ambiguity of the signifier, and advocates listening to the patient's speech (in all its forms) as Freud listened to the dream: as a cipher of sorts, which can yield meaning(s) altogether different from what it presents on its face, if only its letter is followed.

> [The analyst] takes the description of an everyday event as a fable addressed as a word to the wise, a long prosopopeia as a direct interjection, and, contrariwise, a simple slip of the tongue as a highly complex statement, and even the rest of a silence as the whole lyrical development it stands in for. (p. 44)
>
> We must thus take up Freud's work again starting with the *Traumdeutung* to remind ourselves that a dream has the structure of a sentence, or, rather, to keep to the letter of the work, of a rebus—that is, a form of writing ... (p. 57)
>
> [A]nd if [Freud] teaches us to follow the ascending ramification of the symbolic lineage in the text of the patient's free associations, in order to detect the nodal points of its structure at the places where its verbal forms intersect, then it is already quite clear that *symptoms can be entirely resolved in an analysis of language*, because a symptom is itself structured like a language: A symptom is language from which speech must be delivered. (p. 58, emphasis added)

If this is how the analyst is to listen, how then is he to act? This question, and often its apparent lack of an answer, seem to have plagued the proposition of a Lacanian praxis from the beginning. Indeed, another dimension of "Function and Field" was an answer to criticism he had received for his "short sessions," which he argues for as a sort of (re)punctuation of the speech the patient brings to analysis. But we need not embrace this controversial technique in order to understand some of the implications for practice inherent in a language-based approach to psychoanalysis.

The question of implications for practice will guide this book. For the moment, however, I suggest that the mystery of "what Lacanians actually *do*" already begins to be unraveled by the attitude Lacan proposes we take in *listening*, something perhaps too quickly regarded in our everyday way of thinking as passive. Listening, on examination, is not passive at all: The way we listen has direct implications for the other ways we act in any exchange, psychotherapeutic or not. We respond to another person, thereby co-constituting the conversation, the other's "meanings," and any action that is taken in regard to them by the listener or the speaker. This is no less the case in psychoanalysis.

For example, we can look again at the analyst's response to the slip of the tongue above. From this, we can see that the analyst shows an interest in what is actually said, in the *letter* of the patient's speech. He punctuates the syllable that the (ego of) the patient didn't *mean* to say, but that somehow slipped out anyway. By highlighting or punctuating the slip, even with the simple repetition he first utters, the analyst has already acted. This charts a course of conversation in the session markedly different from the one that might have ensued should the analyst have passed the slip over in favor of the intention of the patient's ego-determined *meaning*. In that case, he may have said something like "yes, I know! You're exhausted by the end of the day, what with your long hours at work. It must be very frustrating not to be able to sit back and relax when you get home." Instead, the analyst sees the slip itself as the unconscious Subject (whose intentions are not the same as the ego's) speaking, and follows the letter. He may then pursue the patient's associations to "turn er on," which include "turn her on," reminding the patient of his wife, who does not seem to be sexually interested in him. The patient then hears "turner on" again, and is reminded of Ted Turner, the television magnate whose marriage with Jane Fonda ended in divorce. Our patient remembers that during his parents' divorce, one of his mother's chief complaints seemed to be that his father watched too much television. She often said that this made her feel like a "plain Jane" and that her husband was "more fond o' television" than he was of her.

One stray syllable could yield all this and more, yet without a specific type of attention from the analyst, these connections might go unnoticed and unexplored. Here we see what Lacan refers to as a "refraction" of the signifier into its many contexts for the subject, which can be read not just in a linear way, but also synchronically: One word sounds a number of meanings and associations simultaneously. Lacan employs the metaphor of a musical score with a number of staves, each of which plays simultaneously when the subject speaks. Without making any interpretation of the meaning of the slip, we find by following the letter in our example a "score" that reads something like this:

Turn er on
___
Turn [wife] on
___
Ted Turner/Jane Fonda
___
Divorce
___
Father's watching television leads to mother's anger[4]
___

In one beat of a song playing on the radio, the casual listener may hear a unified tone, while a trained musician may hear in that same beat a number of distinct sounds coming from the bass, the saxophone, the lead guitar, the rhythm guitar, and the drum cymbal. Similarly, while in everyday communication we might hear only a nonsensical slip that seems unimportant, here the "slip of the tongue" becomes "a highly complex statement" whose components can be explored and heard distinctly through the refracting lens of the patient's associations. Just as there are qualitative differences between the way a trained musician and the casual listener will hear music, we find a difference between proper psychoanalytic listening and everyday listening. If the analyst acts on this kind of listening by encouraging the patient to elaborate on those constitutive staves of his score, a conversation that is distinct from the everyday (and that is arguably therapeutic) is bound to result.

Lacan, then, is advocating a radical shift for psychoanalysis away from this everyday conversation, at least insofar as it occurs in the treatment setting. Away from the pursuit of what is constructed as beyond language, away from the ego as a master of reality, away from a "two-body psychology" that runs on ineffable interpersonal contact. Those, he says, who take these latter as the centerpieces of psychoanalysis "are the very people who, making their objective what lies beyond language, react to analysis' 'Don't touch' rule by a sort of obsession. If they keep going in that

[4] A similarly structured example is to be found in Fink (2004, pp. 90–91).

direction, I dare say the last word in transference reaction will be sniffing each other" (1953/2002, p. 57).

Lacan sees these trends as aspects of a case of mistaken identity: the belief that Freud's work occurred in the register of the imaginary. With his "return to Freud," Lacan asserts that this mistake runs the risk of leaving behind the essence of psychoanalysis—the curative properties of the symbolic register, of language itself. The stock he puts in this claim is unmistakable when we read the words "symptoms can be entirely resolved in an analysis of language."[5]

Hence Lacan's (1953/2002) advice to a young psychoanalyst: "Do crossword puzzles" (p. 266).

[5] This is reflective of Lacan's early characterization of psychoanalysis, which was reworked and added to a number of times throughout his career. Generally speaking, this book takes for its theoretical point of departure Lacan's early work.

2

Evidence and Psychotherapy

A History of Case Histories

FREUD'S RESEARCH INTO LANGUAGE AND THERAPY

Lacan made the case that pathology for Freud obeyed the rules of a linguistic/symbolic structure, and that attention to that structure and its individual contents allowed the patient and the analyst to "read" what it was the patient's symptoms *said*. Freud (1900) did in fact note in his investigations of these symbolic "structures" that "unraveling them coincides with removing them" (p. 100). Indeed, language was at issue from the very beginning, with Freud and Breuer contending in *Studies on Hysteria* (1895) that the newly discovered "talking cure," as Breuer's patient Anna O. named it, works because "It brings to an end the operative force of the idea which was not abreacted in the first instance, by allowing its strangulated affect to find a way out through speech" (p. 17).

Perhaps more thematic theoretical attention was paid in *Studies on Hysteria* to the concept that the pathogen was a repressed thought or traumatic event that had not been allowed abreaction than was paid to the linguistic structure that pervaded the symptom formation. But the fundamental discovery that language was important, that it was key to the affective discharge, and that it informed the structure of the disease as well as providing a map to the cure, was already present in these studies. In Freud's and Breuer's "Preliminary Communication" to *Studies*, they already refer to a "'symbolic' relation between the precipitating cause and the pathological phenomenon" (p. 3). Freud pursues these symbolic connections in his discussion, for example, of Fraulein Elisabeth Von R. and her discourse on "standing alone," "tak[ing] another step forward," "find[ing] herself on the right footing," and other signifiers Freud sees as key to the genesis (and therefore understanding and resolution) of her symptoms (pp. 135–181).

While the status of Freud's self-analysis as proper "clinical case material" is certainly debatable and problematic in a number of ways, it seems appropriate to include that work here given that it provides an early instance of application of Freud's technique, albeit only to himself. *The Interpretation of Dreams* (1900) brought to the fore the linguistic nature of the unconscious communication of the dream.

Freud (1900) postulates that the dream is nearly identical in structure to the symptom, and that it can be treated psychoanalytically in the same way—symbolically. It is in this work that Freud, invoking James Sully, reclaims the notion of the dream as a meaningful communication from the conventional wisdom of "such authorities as Chaucer, Shakespeare, and Milton" who saw the dream as "utter nonsense." Freud compares it rather to "some letter in a cipher" and a "palimpsest [that] discloses beneath its worthless surface-characters traces of an old and precious communication" (p. 135).

In *The Interpretation of Dreams*, Freud makes the distinction that Lacan was to take up later as the Imaginary and Symbolic registers, a distinction between two ways of seeing (or reading) the dream. Freud likens the images in a dream, which on their face seem nonsensical, to the figures in a rebus, which are meant to be read symbolically for the signifiers they imply and the linguistic connections they make; that is, as constituting a "pictographic script" rather than simply gazed at as mute, meaningless images.

> If we attempted to read these characters [of a rebus] according to their pictorial value instead of according to their symbolic relation we should clearly be led into error. … But obviously we can only form a proper judgment of the rebus if we … instead, try to replace each separate element by a syllable or word that can be represented by that element in some way or other. The words which are put together in this way are no longer nonsensical but may form a poetical phrase of the greatest beauty and significance. A dream is a picture-puzzle of this sort. (p. 278)

As in *Jokes and Their Relation to the Unconscious* (1905b), Freud's thinking here is not limited to the transformation of images into text. Rather, words themselves are also at issue. In figures of speech, alliterations, neologisms, puns, and other peculiarities of language, Freud finds inroads to the meanings of his dreams. At the heart of this interpretive tactic lies Freud's interrogation of the ambiguity of the signifier, which gave rise to his concept of "switch-words" or "verbal bridges": "Words, since they are the nodal points of numerous ideas, may be regarded as predestined to ambiguity; and the neuroses (e.g., in framing obsessions and phobias), no less than dreams, make unashamed use of the advantages thus offered by words for purposes of condensation and disguise" (p. 341).

In his case studies proper, we see Freud's notion that the ambiguity of the word, or signifier, provides a "nodal point" for discovering the meaning of the symptom, take shape with his patients. Two cases that serve as perhaps the best examples of this approach from Freud's work are "Fragments of an Analysis of a Case of Hysteria" (1905a) and "Notes upon a Case of Obsessional Neurosis" (1909). We will examine them briefly with an eye not on interpretation as such, but on the way in which Freud "refracts" his patients' "speech," showing the polyvalence of certain signifiers. What is of interest here is not so much the final outcome or formulation of the case, but the process of using language as a primary model for listening to the patient.

To begin, there is the (in)famous case of Dora, which Freud tells us can be read as a companion piece to *The Interpretation of*

Dreams. The dreams in *Dora* do take up a considerable amount of the author's attention, and we have in its pages the first example of Freud's dream theory as applied clinically. This piece, perhaps more than Freud's other case studies, has received analyses upon meta-analyses, and the criticism of his clinical judgment in this case is well known (see Kahane & Bernheimer, 1990). What makes it of interest presently, however, is the ease with which that text illustrates what Lacan later termed the *symbolic register.* Here, Freud engages often in "following the letter" of his patient in her dreams, rhetoric, symptomatic behaviors, and associations, and the concept of the "switch word" articulated in *The Interpretation of Dreams* continues to be applied with Dora.

The instances of this approach in *Dora* are numerous. One example concerns Dora's discourse (both in her first dream and in her conversations with Freud) about the signifier "jewel case": Her narration of the dream states "Mother wanted to stop and save her jewel-case; but Father said: 'I refuse to let myself and my two children be burnt for the sake of your jewel-case'" (1905a, p. 64). Freud pursues her associations to "jewel-case," which yield that her mother is "very fond of jewelry" (p. 68) and that one year before the dream occurred, she witnessed an argument between her parents over her father having bought her mother a bracelet instead of the pearl drops she had asked for, which Freud hypothesizes Dora takes as a cue to fantasize that, were she in her mother's place, she would "accept it with pleasure" (p. 69). That is, perhaps she would take whatever it is her father offers to put in her mother's jewel-case into her own. Noting that in response to his query about the jewel-case, Dora has "only talked about jewelry and [has] said nothing about a case" (p. 69), which highlights the fact that Herr K. had shortly before the dream given Dora a jewel-case, Freud zeros in on the signifier itself, listening to its ambiguity, and notes that "'jewel-case' ['*Schmuck-kastchen*'] is a favourite expression … for the female genitals" (p. 69).

The map of associations (which, admittedly, seem to have largely been authored by Freud himself) around "jewel-case" is too complex for a meaningful summary to be made here. But what should be clear is that by following the letter of Dora's discourse about the dream, Freud is able to read its overdetermination, seeing in the term "jewel-case" a number of meanings: jewel-case implies the vagina and cleanliness (and therefore dirtiness and wetness, which is again implied by the association of "drops"). This ultimately leads Freud to understand the dream as a complex expression of infantile representations of sexuality, oedipal issues, and unconscious conflict over a wish to yield to Herr K.'s sexual advances.

While Dora has constituted a classical text in the psychoanalytic literature, continues to fuel discourse more than a century later, and certainly provides us with numerous examples in a case-study form of what Lacan advocated as the true discovery of psychoanalysis, Freud himself tells us in his "Prefatory Remarks" that this case is incomplete in three major ways. First, he admits of the "incompleteness of the analysis," which led Freud to reconstitute elements of the case, filling in gaps where he saw fit: "I have restored what is missing," says Freud. Secondly, as we often see in psychoanalytic case histories, technique is largely not discussed, although we can perhaps see evidence of it in his narrative, problematic though the technique implied may be. Rather, Freud saw this case study as an attempt to "demonstrate the intimate structure of a neurotic disorder and the determination of its symptoms," and shied away from muddying the waters with lengthy discussion of psychoanalytic technique (p. 13). Third, Freud brings our attention to the fact that no matter how complete he might make this study, it is only one account of one patient, and must necessarily leave a number of questions open about its subject matter.

To be sure, the case of Dora leaves a number of gaps for the reader, especially the contemporary American reader. Probably most well known is the fact that Dora's was not simply an incomplete, but a *failed* analysis. Freud may have been able to listen in accordance with the theory we are examining here, but what good did it do him, or more to the point, his patient? While Freud's text may call for a sympathetic reading as a clinical example—it is, after all, instructive to the clinician inasmuch as it illustrates some decidedly wrong moves in the analytic situation (Freud's frequent insistence upon his own interpretations, for example)—it perhaps raises more questions than provides answers (see, for example, Kahane & Bernheimer, 1990). Further, the contemporary clinician is rightfully wary of what we may see as misogyny on Freud's part in this case, with his insinuations that Dora was "asking for it" from Herr K. and his obvious privileging of heterosexuality. While Freud was indeed reading his patient's speech as a musical score, as Lacan put it, it remains highly suspect whether Dora was its composer. The case studies in this book take measures to avoid this problem.

The case of the Rat Man, too, provides invaluable examples of the way in which the ambiguous, polyvalent signifier comes to inform and structure the patient's predicament. "Notes Upon a Case of Obsessional Neurosis" (1909) also grants the reader the added comfort that the analysis seems to have been successful, as Freud declares in a 1923 footnote that "[t]he patient's mental health was restored to him by the analysis which I have reported upon in these pages"; unfortunately, "Like so many other young men of value and promise, he perished in the Great War" (p. 249). Hence it is impossible to say whether the treatment's effect would have been a lasting one.

Be that as it may, we once again find Freud constituting neurotic symptoms as a kind of speech in this study. Freud finds that it is perhaps easier to translate the language of the obsessional neurotic than that of the hysteric:

> The language of an obsessional neurosis—the means by which it expresses its secret thoughts—is, as it were, only a dialect of the language of hysteria; but it is a dialect in which we ought to be able to find our way about more easily, since it is more nearly related to the forms of expression adopted by our conscious thought than is the language of hysteria. Above all, it does not involve … hysterical conversion—which can never be fully comprehensible to us. (p. 157)

As in the case of Dora, the examples of Freud "following the letter" in the case of the Rat Man are numerous. The word *Ratten* (rats), which serves as the pivotal word in the "exciting cause" of the Rat Man's symptoms, implies a number of other words, all of which bear directly upon the patient's history and the complex around which his symptoms form. *Ratten* implies the similarly constructed *Raten*, or "installments," a means of repayment, which applies to the Rat Man's own predicament with his *pince-nez* as well as the possibility of his father's repayment of a gambling debt. Indeed, the word to describe a gambler such as his father is *Spielratte*, again bringing "rat" to into the picture.

> Little by little he translated into this language the whole complex of money interests which centered round his father's legacy to him; that is to say, all his ideas connected with that subject were, by way of the verbal bridge "Raten-Ratten" carried over into his obsessional life … he coined himself a regular rat currency. (p. 213)

The Rat Man also connected rats with infectious diseases such as syphilis, which again indicates "all sorts of doubts [the patient had] as to the kind of life his father had led during his term of military service" (p. 214). This in turn implicates the penis, the conduit of syphilitic infection, which is then likened to a worm, which by virtue of the Rat Man's own experience with round worms in his anus leads back to the exciting cause of his symptoms, the story of the torture by means of rats burrowing into the anus of the transgressive man. "Thus," Freud concludes, "the penis significance of rats was based … upon anal erotism" (p. 213).

The syllable *rat* is found in a number of other places germane to the Rat Man's predicament as well, such as the important figure of Frau Hofrat, the verb *heiraten* (to marry), and the association of rats with children, including himself as a child who bit someone.

The psychological function of language (or the linguistic structure of psychology) for the Rat Man (or at least for Freud's conception of him) can be found again in his "principal magic word, which was an apotropaic against every evil" (p. 224). This word was constructed from "the initial letters of the most powerfully beneficent of his prayers," and ended with an "amen." Freud

> could not help noticing that the word was in fact an anagram upon the name of his lady. Her name contained an "s," and this he had put last, that is, immediately before the "amen" at the end. We may say, therefore that by this process he had brought his "Samen" [semen] into contact with the woman he loved ... (p. 224)

We find Freud's attention to language again becoming central in another of the Rat Man's compulsions. Upon noticing, during a vacation, that his "lady" was being lavished with attention by her English cousin, Dick, the Rat Man began experiencing a compulsive need to lose weight by refusing food and running (p. 188). As losing weight equals losing fat, and Dick happens not only to be the name of his love interest's cousin, but also the German word for *fat*, Freud is able to translate the patient's compulsion to get rid of his *fat* rather directly into a substitute for getting rid of *Dick*.[1] Dick, in turn, comes to stand in for the patient's father, since he too stands between the patient and the object of his affection.

The case of the Rat Man, like that of Dora, while illustrating what Lacan found so central to Freud's work, leaves a number of loose ends. First, it is left to the reader's imagination whether the alleviation of the Rat Man's symptoms would have endured were his life not prematurely ended with World War I. But perhaps more germane to my work here is the fact that Freud's writing of both these cases is susceptible to criticisms of its accuracy. Freud recorded the content of his sessions after the fact, often at the end of a day filled with patients, as he shied away from taking notes during sessions since the "withdrawal of the physician's attention does the patient more harm than can be made up for by any increase in the accuracy that may be achieved in the reproduction

[1] Unfortunately, Freud does not give us a sense of the patient's familiarity with English, which is unfortunate given the fact of the genital connotation of *Dick*, which would lead, through the signifier *Rat* back to his father. *Dick* began to be used in this fashion around 1890.

of his case history" (1909, p. 159). Be that as it may, given the nature of what is at issue in this research (that is, the "letter" of the patient's speech), it is of some importance to maintain as accurate an account as possible of what the patient says in the session.

Further, Freud was in a professional position markedly different from my own. Not unlike Lacan after him, much of Freud's energy was spent furthering the cause of his new treatment, psychoanalysis, making it palatable and promising to its potential consumers (Roazen, 1995; Roustang, 1990). This need to propagate psychoanalysis arguably had an effect upon the case histories he wrote. Selection of what material is included is always at issue in a narrative case history, and when that selection is accompanied by a rather grand political agenda, we must exercise at least some caution in accepting the story we are told.

LACANIAN CASE STUDIES

If we are looking for examples of a Lacanian approach to the patient's language, where better to look than case studies written by Lacan? If they existed, we certainly would. However, with the exception of a very brief mention of his work with an obsessive patient in "The Direction of the Treatment and the Principles of its Power" (1961/2002, pp. 630–633) and a transcript of an interview he performed with a psychotic patient (Schneiderman, 1980, pp. 19–41), Lacan left us no examples of his own clinical work. Rather, he confined himself to commentary on the cases of other analysts, especially those he wished to critique, but also those of Freud, whom he revered in his own way (see, for example, Lacan, 1988a).

While Lacan himself does not, properly speaking, provide us with case studies of his own, we are furnished with some examples of his students' work. A volume edited and translated by Stuart Schneiderman, *Returning to Freud* (1980), provides most of them: no less than 13 case examples contributed by the students of Lacan in the areas of neurosis, psychosis, and perversion. By and large, these cases integrate the approach to language discussed here, but at the same time place the signifier in the larger context of Lacan's major diagnostic structures and other aspects of his theory.

Yet these cases, as they have been written, unfortunately serve somewhat to lend credence to an image of a Lacanian clinical approach as distinctly unclinical. Freud once confessed that his case studies "read like short stories and that, as one might say, they lack the serious stamp of science" (Freud & Breuer, 1895). But the liberties Freud took in his case histories pale in comparison to those taken by Lacan's students. A kinder way to put this would be to say, with Yael Goldman (2004), that the cases presented by Leclaire, Tostain, Shaetzel, and others in this volume assume a "sophisticated working knowledge of Lacanian theory" (p. 47). The degree of abstraction in these cases is arguably of a piece with Lacan's own writing, and one imagines that like Lacan himself, its authors harbored some resistance toward writing "for idiots." Unfortunately, "idiots" is a term that seems to encompass not only those who are not well-versed in Lacan, but those who are not already enthused about his theories. Therefore, the audience for these case histories is extremely limited. And they, like Freud's case histories, bear the mark of the politics of an ideological movement. Lacan's students were invested in promoting Lacan, both in their clinical approach and their writing style, the latter being perhaps a self-defeating measure.

Kareen Ror Malone and Stephen Friedlander have also contributed to the effort of clearer communication about Lacanian theory with their *The Subject of Lacan: A Lacanian Reader for Psychologists* (2000). This volume of theoretical and clinical writing aims to promote a "cross cultural dialogue" wherein Lacan might be taken up within the larger American psychological discourse. While the book contains one section entitled "Lacan and the Clinic," it remains rather theoretical overall, including only three case examples, none of which can be said to be "in depth" and only one of which (Mario Beira's "Reflections on Lacan's View of Interpretation") deals briefly with attention to the letter of the patient's speech. The essays generally describe the theoretical position one takes in regard to a clinical stance, but fall short when it comes to actually illustrating that stance concretely and comprehensively.

More accessible to an English-speaking audience of psychological practitioners is the work of Bruce Fink, who has provided the reader with several instances of case material in *Fundamentals of Psychoanalytic Technique* (2007) and *A Clinical Introduction to Lacanian Psychoanalysis* (1997). In this latter text, which "assume[s] no prior knowledge of Lacan's work" and "attempts to provide a sorely lacking meeting place for theory and practice" (p. xi), Fink uses two of his own case examples to illustrate Lacan's diagnostic categories of hysteria and obsession, and demonstrates perversion and psychosis using cases by Tostain and Schaetzel (both of which appear in *Returning to Freud,* Schneiderman, 1980). Again, while the "play of the signifier" is given a good deal of attention here, the cases themselves remain in the service of illustrating Lacan's diagnostic system, and occur in a text that is primarily devoted to pedagogy of Lacanian theory in general. Therefore, they are necessarily limited in breadth and depth as case studies.

Fink (2003) has also provided clinicians with a case study of perversion, "Lacanian Psychoanalysis and Fetishism," which goes into much greater detail around the "signifying contributions" to the constitution of the patient's boot fetish. He demonstrates with great facility the way in which "boot" comes to serve to prop up the patient's own genitalia through a series of semantic moves, integrating masculinity and femininity through signifiers such as "butt," "thumb," "root," "tube," "booty," "boob," and others. Unlike the case studies by Tostain, Schaetzel, and Leclaire, this piece speaks to an audience of American practitioners without assuming prior familiarity with Lacan, nor does it come across as the work of a zealous disciple. Yet, as Freud pointed out about Dora, it is only one case study. Secondly, the analysand discussed in this case came to Fink already quite well aware of Freudian and Lacanian theory, making references during the course of his analysis to his "primal scene," his "mother's *jouissance*," and the "*vagina dentata*." As Fink points out, "the analysand originally chose [Fink] as his analyst due to his preexisting interest in Lacan's work" (p. 59).

The use of such a patient for a case study may be subject to the criticism that the treatment simply serves to prop up a patient's already Lacanian identity, or even that it further enables his already strong intellectual defenses. Perhaps such an analysand is too willing to produce what the analyst wants: slips of the tongue, ambiguous turns of phrase, and so on. Hence there may be a place for Lacanian case studies that involve patients who are *not* already expert in Lacan, who do not show up for the first session ready with an arsenal of psychoanalytic jargon, puns, and double entendres to plumb the depths of their *jouissance*. Can a Lacanian approach be effective with those who are not "in the know?"

Furthermore, Fink is a Lacanian psychoanalyst, just as the authors of the case studies I've discussed above were all analysts. If we are justified in wondering whether a patient who is not already something of a Lacanian can benefit from a Lacanian approach to therapy, we may also wonder what it might look like for a nonanalyst to implement Lacan's ideas clinically.

A PSYCHOTHERAPIST'S VIEW OF LACAN

I am not a psychoanalyst, although I consider the psychotherapy that I do to be psychoanalytic in nature and heavily influenced by Lacanian theory. Rather, I am a therapist with a background in existential, phenomenological, humanistic, and psychodynamic approaches, all of which informed (and continue to inform) my work before I became interested in psychoanalysis. My knowledge about Lacan was gleaned outside of psychoanalytic institutes, in doctoral-level coursework, study groups, conferences, and clinical supervision from those who are experts. In a word, my clinical work is psychotherapy and not analysis.

Starting from there, this book looks to explore several questions. What might an attunement to language, as Lacan advocates it, mean for psychotherapy as directed by a nonanalyst? If the clinician follows the letter in the patient's speech, including the speech of his symptoms, fantasies, and dreams, how does this affect his case formulation and interventions, and the overall direction the course of treatment will take? More specifically, how does this approach look within psychotherapies that occur in a more traditionally psychodynamic frame (once or twice per week sessions at a fixed length of 50 minutes), and with clients who are not already familiar with the tenets of psychoanalysis, much less Lacanian psychoanalysis?

Each of the chapters that follow includes what I hope is accessible theoretical discussion of the concepts informing my approaches to Lacanian case formulation and intervention, which I then link to the case histories and formulations themselves. It is my hope that this book will provide a useful point of reference and opportunity for further thinking and debate for other practitioners by illustrating the interpretation and appropriation of a Lacanian-psychoanalytic approach to listening and intervention by a psychotherapist.

CLINICAL RESEARCH AND EVIDENCE-BASED PRACTICE

A student of mine recently told me about how she fired her therapist, Dr. Emanuel. Having learned about the current trends in psychotherapy surrounding "empirically supported treatments," she decided that she would ask Dr. Emanuel what manual he was using in her treatment. "None," he replied. The patient, in her dismay, left treatment in short order, abandoning Emanuel for a manual.

How did that happen?

We can find a number of potential answers in the therapeutic relationship, or the therapist's competence, or the patient's anxiety level. But we have the benefit of having been told already—it was about research, and indirectly, then, about the power the positivist research paradigm has gained over the practice of psychotherapy.

The positivist conviction that there is one objective truth and one way to find it (experimental method) still dominates psychology long after some of the "harder" sciences have begun to note their uneasiness in its embrace. The observer effect (that the observer changes the observed simply by observing it) has been but one way in which physics, for example, has distanced itself from the notion that reality exists in pure form apart from our perception. Yet psychology's methods have by and large continued to assume a pristine, objective order to the universe—and to human experience and behavior themselves—that exists independently of, well, human experience and behavior. These assumptions are visible in experimental method, which used to dictate that the experimenter was set apart from his experiment. After Rosenthal (1966), this illusion was given up, but only inasmuch as psychological science has come to insist that that whatever effects the researcher has upon his research must be "controlled for."

Similarly, our independent variable must be the same each time we study it. This becomes problematic when we attempt to study psychotherapy, the meeting of two human beings who engage in a discussion about subjectivity. To apply experimental method to this field, the psychotherapy being studied—the independent variable—must be rendered identical over multiple trials. This requirement is answered by the relatively recent introduction of the treatment manual, which is often constructed for the purpose of studying the treatment it manualizes. Manuals vary in their specificity, but some are really quite specific and leave little room for what the naïve might think of as "expertise." Another colleague comes to mind here, who told me that given its scientific (and therefore highly credible) manualization, "a monkey should be able to do" his brand of cognitive-behavioral therapy. He was quite proud of this.

If the numbers bear out the idea that the application of the manual (with as little human interference or variation as possible) has helped reduce the presenting complaint in question (the dependent variable), we have the birth of an "empirically supported" treatment, which fits with the broader "evidence-based" movement in psychotherapy and medicine.

That is, we have a treatment that qualifies under the dominant discourse as legitimate.

From this standpoint, my student was utterly reasonable in her objection and decision to leave. If her therapist was not following a manual, then it would seem there is no "evidence basis" for his treatment. Why continue with a treatment akin to prescribing mud pies for strep throat?

But, if Dr. Emanuel wants the legitimacy that his patients demand and deserve, then he should submit his therapy to empirical research! So let's say he sets about doing just that. The first problem is that he must translate the entirety of his expertise into an easily digestible manual that gives specific instructions for every eventuality, keeping variations across therapists to an absolute minimum. Let us say that Dr. Emanuel writes his manual. Yet now he discovers, inevitably, that simply by virtue of being manualized, the treatment is no longer the same kind of activity that Dr. Emanuel engaged in with my student. Bohart, O'Hara, and Leitner (1998) made a compelling case to this effect, arguing that to study many therapies via the randomized clinical trial *is to deface those therapies so dramatically that what is being studied is something altogether different.* Imagine, as Bohart et al. do, manualizing humanistic therapy, which holds as core values authenticity and spontaneity!

Also problematic is the longstanding divide in American psychology, going back to the days of Boring (see O'Donell, 1979), between the clinician and the researcher. Elements of psychotherapy that are tested in laboratory settings are often created there by researchers who have precious little clinical experience or investment. The result is a body of research that seems irrelevant and unappealing to many practicing clinicians.

I am not the first to complain about this state of affairs. A number of authors (see, for example, Bergin, 1997; Beutler, 1997; Bohart, 2000; Walsh, 2004) have critiqued the current trend toward manualization and the dominant position given to the randomized controlled trial (RCT) in clinical research. Russell Walsh (2004) argues that the dominant "rules of the [research] game," with their "insistence on objectivity," lead to research that "produces a form of knowledge inaccessible or irrelevant to the practicing clinician" (p. 3). In fact, Walsh points out that "surveys of practicing therapists find that much of published psychotherapy research is rarely consulted and ... case studies and personal experience are more likely to influence a therapist's actions" (p. 5). Thus, we are left with a "widely acknowledged gap between research and clinical practice" (p. 3; see also Bickman, 1999; Goldman, 2004; Godfried & Wolfe, 1996).

Just as the trend in Lacanian literature has been a predilection for theory over praxis, psychology research in general has often, by virtue of narrowly constraining what type of evidence is admissible, left the reading clinician lacking any sense of a relevance to what she does, which involves a specific interaction between individuals. The natural-scientific discourse of American psychology research has left the clinician with a stark choice: continue his own work without much help from the researcher, or adopt a manualized approach that consigns the individual he is treating and the unique content of the treatment itself to irrelevance.

In the United Kingdom, the "practice-based evidence" movement, an answer to the more dominant "evidence-based practice" school, has noticed this problem, and has emphasized the method of observational studies of *in vivo* psychotherapy, rather than therapies created for the purpose of experimentation, thus improving the claim to external validity (Barkham et al., 2001). While encouraging, Barkham's emphasis on external validity is hardly new. Proponents of qualitative research have long been pointing to external (real-world) validity as the weakness of quantitative methods and the strength of their own approach. Happily, these researchers have gained a stronger voice in recent years within American psychology, and an even more impressive influence upon British thinking, yet the experimental method and the RCT continue to hold sway, especially in the United States. Frequently, we see qualitative research as a supplement to research that is primarily quantitative, but not used as a primary methodology in journals like the *American Psychologist*.

While there is much to be learned from the experimental method, I find it valuable as a clinician to discuss the relationship between theory and practice in an "externally valid" way, and I know that many of my fellow clinicians feel the same. From a more collective point of view, Bickman (1999) points out that the divergence between researchers and practitioners has resulted in a discourse that has in fact become "unresponsive to societal needs" (p. 96), and calls upon practitioners to reclaim the practice of speaking about what they do.

Oddly enough, even Lacan, who as I have mentioned is noted for his reticence about his own clinical case material as well as for his theoretical obfuscation, calls for the need to explicate "what we do when we are doing psychoanalysis" (1988a). Further, Lacan (1953/2002) declares, "If psychoanalysis can become a science (for it is not yet one) and if it is not to degenerate in its technique (and perhaps this has already happened), we must rediscover the meaning of its experience" (p. 57). Surely, part of what is required to do this is an explication of concrete instances of practice.

So while I respect science, and find the contributions of experimental method valuable in their way, I propose that reading clinicians might be more appreciative of a discussion of therapy. Especially when that therapy is of a type that is not well known, they might like a description of what the clinician actually does and why he does it. So here, I am attempting to speak about what I have done.

Since Breuer and Freud, the tradition of the practitioner researcher has by and large adopted the vehicle of the clinical case study. This approach carries the stigma of "subjectivity" and the related potential for numerous pitfalls, which I will discuss later. Yet when performed with rigor, it remains an effective method of articulating the ways in which a specific clinical approach affects the course of a psychotherapy (Goldman, 2004; Spinelli, 1997; Yin, 2003).

In discussions with colleagues about therapeutic praxis, it is commonplace for us to use examples of our own clinical experiences to illustrate an idea. When a clinician speaks, isn't it proper that he speak about his own clinical experience? How did he listen, how did he intervene, how did he formulate the case? It seems to me that we must discuss our practice in concrete terms if our professional communications are to be much more than abstract philosophical exercises or empty articulations of "manualized" approaches. To paraphrase Lacan (1953/2002), if we are to investigate the meaning of the experience of psychotherapy, we must attend to the details of its content.

Wanting to make a useful contribution to clinical discourse as a speaking clinician, then, I am offering clinical case studies of my own former patients. These case studies primarily seek to illustrate in detail the impact that a Lacanian approach to the patient's language has upon the listening, and thereby upon the formulation and interventions, of the clinician; an impact that I posit is unique in the world of psychotherapy.

A NOTE ON RIGOR AND REFLEXIVITY

Another charge that can be brought against the method of the case study concerns author/practitioner's subjectivity. My attention is bound, not only by virtue of considerations of confidentiality, but also by various aspects of my own subjectivity, to have been selective as I wrote these case studies, just as it no doubt was in my approach to treatment. These problems are probably unavoidable, but some rigor can be brought to the project to balance the dangers they present.

My unconscious fantasies, my fears and desires, for example, surely played a role in my presentation of the case material. (What, for example, might influence my choice of a pseudonym for a particular patient? Why have I chosen to discuss some themes over others?) As a psychotherapist, I try to make a practice of maintaining as much awareness as possible of my own countertransference, exploring it as I think about my patients during sessions, on my own, and in supervision. Similarly, I scrutinized my countertransference as I wrote the cases, both explicitly in the text where appropriate, and reflexively in the writing and thinking processes.

The clinical method I illustrate in this book—the analysis of the patient's language to its letter—will itself function as a point of departure for methodological rigor. My interventions with these patients were generally *spoken*, and therefore in my discussion of the cases, I followed them "to the letter" as much as possible and discussed their various implications. Similarly, I did, after all, *write* about these cases and the words I chose lend themselves to a scrutiny similar to that which I brought to the cases themselves. I have attended to this as part of the writing process, but I have not made extensive explorations of my own language in the text itself, as I feel this would distract from the primary focus. Certainly, however, my own language can be taken up by the reader in ways that I may (or may not) have missed as I wrote.

Subjectivity itself, the apparent weakness of this method, can also be taken up as one of its greatest strengths. In much of psychotherapy research the clinician's motivations go largely unexamined (Bergin, 1997; Beutler, 1997; Bohart, 2000; Walsh, 2004). Treatment modalities are often taken up as somehow divorced from philosophical orientation, training, and theoretical stance. The nature of case study research, however, can be such that motivation in terms of these variables is an indispensable part of the narrative, and I intend to be rigorous in my explication of these elements. This book is an exercise in applied theory, and as such necessarily entails discussion and explanation of theoretical constructs, as well as of the specific ways in which I integrated them into the cases under examination. All of this will be taken up as the somewhat experimental work of a clinician with training in several theoretical models, and from this point of view I will explore interventional failures and successes, as well as those moments that I may be unable to categorize as either.

This book aims to contribute to an emerging body of literature that has set out to create a voice for Lacanian approaches to psychotherapy in the United States. This project, taken up by Dor, Fink, Goldman, Nobus, Schneiderman, and Ror Malone, among others, is a recent undertaking and still leaves a number of gaps. Most notably, these authors (with the exception of Goldman, 2004) have often focused on theoretical elucidation of Lacan's concepts without explicit attention to their clinical application.

Each of the chapters that follow includes what I intend to be accessible theoretical discussion of the concepts informing my approaches to case formulation and intervention, which I then link to the case histories and formulations themselves. It is my hope that this book will provide a useful point of reference and opportunity for further thinking and debate for other practitioners by illustrating the interpretation and appropriation of a Lacanian-psychoanalytic approach to listening and intervention by a psychotherapist.

ABOUT THE CASE STUDIES

The following case studies are written and arranged with several organizing principles in mind. While I stay focused on one overarching theme, following patients' speech to the letter as a therapeutic practice, I will place that theme in dialogue with several aspects of psychotherapy which may already be somewhat familiar to the reading clinician, thus attempting to narrow the gap between the more commonly held goals of American psychodynamic therapy and some possible interpretations and uses of Lacanian theory.

The case studies begin by discussing a beginning. A first dilemma with which the psychodynamic or psychoanalytic therapist must come to grapple anew for each patient is the question of how that patient can come to see his own situation from a new enough perspective to begin to truly invest himself in the project of change. How can we be of use to the patient in moving toward a questioning of his own history, and seeing his lived world less as a given and more as one possibility among others, to which his own psychology has contributed? Many psychodynamic and psychoanalytic therapists see such a capacity to dwell in what Winnicott calls "potential space," where there is room to experiment with one's narrative and experience, as necessary to the larger project of therapy. Yet it is often no small task to help guide the patient to this attitude. Some clinicians, such as Davenloo (1990), have favored an aggressive approach that relies heavily upon interpretations to challenge defenses, thereby acting to engage the patient in therapeutic discourse with speed and intensity. Others, such as Davies (2004), Maroda (1999, 2001), and Renik (1999), prefer the engagement in and exploration of interpersonal enactments as a means of engaging the patient in psychological reflection.

In Chapter 3, I discuss Lacan's "Seminar on 'The Purloined Letter'" (1966), and take from it the notion that neither aggressive interpretation of what the therapist sees as the patient's unconscious, nor the mutual acting out of the patient's unconscious past, are necessary to the opening up of "potential space." Rather, my reading of that paper suggests that the patient can be engaged this way on the basis of the ambiguity of his language. The case study I present in Chapter 3 is an exploration of how an almost microscopic attention to the letter of the patient's speech seems to have had the effect of helping the patient become a more "productive" participant in psychotherapy, and moving him toward greater reflection within the therapeutic process. This chapter also examines the question of what the psychotherapist deems important enough in the patient's discourse and behavior to warrant therapeutic attention.

Another concern that is common to many psychodynamic and psychoanalytic therapists is how to approach the transference. In Chapter 4, I closely examine Lacan's "Aggressiveness in Psychoanalysis" (1948/2002) and extract from it some guiding principles for a therapeutic approach to transference. I follow this reading with a highly detailed discussion of several moments of aggressive transference in the case of my patient, Eric. I then illustrate my attempt to implement attention to the letter of Eric's speech in the service of following the principles that I interpret Lacan to be articulating in the previously mentioned text. Overall, I attempt to reconcile theory that is outside the mainstream with a goal more commonly held by American clinicians: using the transference to serve the therapeutic process, rather than to derail it.

Chapter 5 addresses a concept that has been at the heart of much disagreement in the psychoanalytic and critical theory communities: that of the phallus. Because of their direct relationship with the construction of sexuality and gender and their attendant dynamics of social power, the patient's fantasies and experience of himself vis-à-vis some notion of the phallus are of central importance to any psychotherapy. Lacan's comments on his own notion of the phallus are explored in Chapter 5, and applied to Steve's therapeutic work, once again via attention to the letter of his speech.

Chapter 6 explores the related question of how the clinician is to aid the patient in beginning to articulate desire when that desire seems to have been negated. Psychodynamic and psychoanalytic therapists may often find themselves sitting with patients who seem to have abdicated all desire of their own, attempting instead to divine that of other people in an attempt to psychologically survive. This kind of patient presents a special challenge to the psychotherapist, who of course does not wish merely to repeat this pattern with the patient, but perhaps to help him find more agency in the articulation of his own desire. Lacanian theory has addressed this character structure as that of hysteria. I attempt to take the work that has been done by Lacanian theorists Bruce Fink and Colette Soler and apply it to detailed glimpses of my clinical work with Caroline, who seemed to fit the character structure in question. Once again, the letter of Caroline's speech forms the centerpiece of the therapy.

Because this last case lends itself so easily to a discussion of countertransference, I engage in some discussion of how that phenomenon might be a help or a hindrance in a Lacanian conception of psychotherapy. I recount some of my own countertransferential processes in this therapy, and how I attempted to use them constructively and in accordance with the principles I outlined previously.

So, questions that guide the work of many clinicians form the themes of this book: engagement in "potential space" and discursive productivity; therapeutic approach to the transference; questions of gender, power, and the phallus; drawing out the patient's ownership of his desire; and how we are to make use of countertransference. For each issue, I attempt to bring Lacanian theory to bear, but I limit that attempt to the use of the letter of the patient's speech (one detail among many facets of Lacanian theory). Further, woven throughout each chapter are other major questions currently at issue in the psychoanalytic and psychodynamic communities, such as the nature of the unconscious, the meaning of the therapeutic relationship, the use of the therapist's power, and the style and timing of interpretation.

3

Strength in Letters

> Language hands down its sentence to those who know how to hear it.
>
> —**Lacan (1966/2006, p. 16)**

"THE PURLOINED LETTER"

Not long ago during a discussion about Lacan, a colleague remarked to me that she could not afford to "be thinking about the signifier and the signified" when her clearer and more pressing duty was to "be present with" her patient. And indeed, the premises I have outlined in Chapter 1's discussion of Lacan's "Function and Field" (1953/2002) concerning the linguistic nature of the unconscious and the prospect of a treatment that can render symptoms "entirely resolved in an analysis of language," may strike the reading clinician as too bold, or even somewhat absurd. To base one's clinical practice on these ideas may require a certain strength of faith in an extremely academic, theoretical, counterintuitive, and opaque (quasi-)philosophical system. Moreover, to hold our understanding of this system in mind at all times during clinical work would seem to require of the clinician a level of abstract thinking that is alien to the more immediate, human encounter with the patient, which has become central to much of the current psychodynamic literature.

So goes the argument between much of American psychoanalytic thinking and that of Lacan, whose retorts to the more relational positions of Balint and the ego psychologists I have discussed previously. But I'd like to suggest that while Lacan is a difficult writer and theoretician, the mode of clinical operation suggested by his theory may not, in fact, be the hyperintellectualized waste of time that we may be inclined to perceive it to be. In fact, rather than locking our understanding of what the patient brings us into a useless abstraction, and rather than removing our conceptualizations too many degrees from the obvious and intuitive to be of much practical help, we might argue that Lacan's approach does just the opposite, and *reclaims* the obvious.

We should be careful not to assume that some psychodynamic theory, by virtue of appearing simpler and more accessible, or by virtue of drawing out strong emotional responses in the reader or the patient, is operating on principles that are in fact simple or straightforward at all. Even if it is, its apparent intuitive and simple nature does not make it any more noble or correct than any other set of propositions. Further, there is no guarantee that simple theories make for a simpler life for the patient, one that is less cluttered and weighed down by the painful complexity of her symptoms. Similarly, the complexity of Lacan's writing and the theoretical vocabulary that emerges in its applications does not preclude the possibility that it can inform powerful and pragmatically helpful experiences in psychotherapy, thus simplifying the life of the patient with whom it is used. We in America seem to have a bias that calls for this reminder, often equating the apparently simple with the morally superior and the apparently complex with the morally inferior.

How does Lacan reclaim the obvious in our clinical work? In the first section of his "Seminar on 'The Purloined Letter'" (1966/2006, pp. 6–30), Lacan uses the famous story by Edgar Allan Poe (1845) to illustrate (among a number of other things) the proposition that psychoanalysis can do its detective work in a mode that stays attuned always to the obvious, to the manifest contents of the patient's discourse, wagering that the mysteries that drive the symptom are hidden there, in plain sight.

Poe's story concerns two detectives: The first, the prefect of police, has been retained by the queen to find an incriminating letter that was stolen from her by a minister who is holding it for blackmailing purposes, as it were. The prefect has searched the apartments of the minister with the help of his entire police force for a number of months, apparently leaving no stone unturned. They have looked in every conceivable hiding place, "running the gamut from hidden desk drawers to removable tabletops, from the unstitched upholstery of chairs to their hollowed-out legs, and from the back side of the quicksilvering of mirrors to the thickness of book bindings" (Lacan, 1966/2006, p. 15), all to no avail. The prefect then visits a second sleuth, Dupin, and expresses his exasperation with the case. Dupin, the cleverer of the two, suggests that the prefect has missed the letter because its hiding place is "too self-evident" (p. 15). Dupin, of course, retrieves the letter easily, and in the process extracts a sum of money from the prefect for having done so.

How does he do it? During an ostensibly casual visit to the minister, Dupin spots the letter sitting in plain sight in the minister's pasteboard card rack. The letter is crumpled, ripped nearly in two, and readdressed to the minister himself, in order not to give away the fact that it was "purloined" in the first place, yet it is also stamped with his seal. Examining (from behind colored glasses that hide the activity of his eyes) the ways in which the paper was worn, Dupin decides that the letter has simply been turned inside out and readdressed. As he continues his visit, he commits the appearance of the letter to memory, and purposely "forgets" a snuffbox as he leaves. At home, he constructs a similar document, and when he returns for the snuffbox, switches the two.

The letter has been hidden in plain sight. It has not been buried, stuffed in a hollow chair leg, hidden in a mirror, or placed between the pages of a book—all elaborate ruses that the prefect has been trained to expect. Rather, it has been made to look unimportant, carelessly stuffed in a card rack, its dirty and ripped condition "suggestive of a design to delude the beholder into an idea of the worthlessness of the document" (Poe, 1845, p. 469).

In his commentary, Lacan seems to be suggesting that the unconscious content that drives the symptom is hidden in much the same way: It is there to be found by those who know how to look (or listen) for it, and this involves being suspicious of that which asks to be taken for granted. In thinking about the unconscious this way, Lacan evokes (and indeed explicitly mentions) Heidegger, whose phenomenology aimed to bring out what is latent in a phenomenon not by performing some kind of archaeology, but by attending to what is not currently being attended to, as his elucidation of the Greek *alethea* attests to in both form and content (Heidegger, 1962). Traditional readings of Freud, as well as Freud himself (1909), have likened psychoanalysis to an archaeological process, but Lacan implies that unconscious contents are made invisible not so much by being buried beneath the ego as by being *displaced*, much as the queen's letter goes through a series of displacements in Poe's story. "What is hidden," Lacan (1966) says, "is never but what is not in its place, as a call slip says of a volume mislaid in a library. And even if the book were on an adjacent shelf or in the next slot, it would be hidden there, however visible it may seem there" (p. 17).

The purloined letter of Poe's story is for Lacan analogous to the letter of the patient's discourse: the signifier. As discussed in Chapter 1, it is the letter of speech to which Lacan says the analyst must attend, since it is there that the unconscious manifests itself, or rather it is the letter that manifests the unconscious. The unconscious speaks, but does so in a cryptic way that involves the displacement of the signifier (the letter), to positions in which it appears to the casual listener as unimportant, in order to "delude the beholder into an idea of the worthlessness of the document." Hence Lacan suggests that the analyst become practiced in the art of finding these displaced signifiers, not necessarily in the "depths" that are suggested by various incarnations of "depth psychology"—the contents of which are, in fact, theoretical constructions of which we rarely if ever see any direct evidence—but in the letter of the speech we actually hear, the analog of the paper in the minister's card rack.

Yet in attending to the (displaced) letter of the patient's speech, our end is not to come to own it, to somehow hold onto it and the power that having gained "the answer" to the patient's problem might confer on us. Rather, it is to return the letter to the patient, having helped to loosen it from the bonds of the repressive mechanism that has held the patient captive to his symptom until now, "blackmailing" the patient, just as the minister blackmails the queen by immobilizing her letter. Indeed, the letter itself—by having been thus immobilized—comes to have an unpleasant power over the minister, too, who finds himself effectively blackmailed by his own act of blackmail (Lacan, 1966/2006, pp. 23, 29).

In Poe's story, the letter is a threat to the ego identities of several people, among them the queen to whom it was originally addressed. Whatever the contents of the letter, we know that she needs to hide it from the king, which shows us that the person she is supposed to be (her ego identity), the loyal queen, is no longer in agreement with the person she *is* (her subjectivity), since her loyalty is sullied by hiding the letter from the king. She therefore (dis)places the letter on a table in the presence of the minister and the king in order to maintain the appearance of propriety and harmony with her ego identity, making the letter look unimportant. The minister notices the ruse, however, and displaces the letter yet again by switching it with one of his own in full view of the queen, who can do nothing about it, since to protest would be to risk giving away what she is trying to hide from the king. Now, the minister gains power from having done this—the power to destroy the queen's standing (ego) by revealing the letter. But what has happened in the meantime is that he has thereby staked his own ego on the notion of having just this power, and he can therefore never actually use the letter, since to do so would also be to give up the power he has over the queen, thereby ceasing to be the ego he has become. The letter is therefore stuck with him, and he is stuck with the letter.

This being the case, the displaced, stuck letter begins to drive the behavior (the symptoms?) not just of the minister who has to go to great lengths to maintain appearances, but also of the queen, who has enlisted the entire police force to save her from blackmail, and finally of the prefect of police, who spends his nights obsessively examining the minister's home for hollowed-out chair legs and failing at every turn. In a move that Minuchin might have appreciated, Poe shows us that all those complicit in this "repression" of the letter, then, become symptomatic. Even the prefect, who does not see his complicity, is made to suffer.

Lacan (1966/2006), in a play on words, refers to this letter, which has been diverted from the path it was originally set on, and that is now stuck, as "a letter *en souffrance*," which figuratively translated means "awaiting delivery or unclaimed" (p. 21). The literal translation of the term, however, is a "suffering letter." But Lacan points out that "while the letter may be *en souffrance*, they [the characters] are the ones who shall suffer from it. By passing beneath its shadow, they become its reflection" (p. 21).

Just as the letter in Poe's story comes to dominate the actions of these characters, the displaced signifier of the unconscious comes to dominate the patient's behavior via the signifying symptom. Lacan says:

> Such is the signifier's answer, beyond all significations: "You believe you are taking action when I am the one making you stir at the bidding of the bonds with which I weave your desires. Thus do the latter grow in strength and multiply in objects, bringing you back to the fragmentation of your rent childhood." (p. 29)

What if the queen were able to freely read her letter, and had no need of hiding it? What if the minister had not staked his identity upon taking it hostage? The ensuing symptoms would never have appeared, of course. Analogously, we might take Lacan to be implying that by putting the signifier *en souffrance* back into conscious play we can aid the person in the therapy room to become less unconsciously dominated by it, less compelled by symptoms that "grow in strength and multiply in objects" in the service of keeping it stuck, and instead become able to speak more freely, able to find and use (and perhaps therefore defuse) what has been displaced, what hides in obvious places.

The following case study is an exploration of what it might mean for the clinician to employ Lacan's emphasis upon the "function and field of speech and language" as they apply to psychoanalysis (as discussed in the previous chapter) by attuning ourselves, like Dupin, to what is hidden in plain sight—the letter of the patient's audible speech. This case is intended as an introduction to the way in which attention to the patient's speech can further the greater therapeutic process by helping the patient to engage in reflection, interrogate his history, and be able to more fully articulate the material that has brought him to therapy in the first place. Unlike the cases that follow, therefore, this case discussion will be relatively brief, focusing upon points at which attention to the letter opened up new doors in the therapy.

THE CASE OF JIM

Clinical Background

Jim, a 30-year-old electrician, referred himself to therapy complaining of feeling "*stuck*"[1] in his life, and "inept as an adult." He was ambivalent about his career and his primary romantic relationship, and worried that in both domains he was not being "*productive*" enough, which compounded his sense of ineptitude. He felt that psychotherapy might be a way of improving his self-understanding, and thereby remedy his ambivalence, making him a more productive boyfriend and worker. Jim had had no prior psychological treatment or counseling of any kind, and

[1] In this chapter, the reader will notice that a number of Jim's words are italicized. I have added this emphasis to highlight that these words are of particular interest to the case in question, and not to indicate any emphasis by Jim.

while he had become briefly acquainted with Freud in an introductory psychology class, did not have an extensive knowledge of psychoanalysis, to say nothing of Lacan.

Jim also suffered from a self-described "phobia" since about the age of 7. He experienced frequent panic attacks in bathrooms, which were driven by thoughts that he might have a heart attack while defecating.

His difficulties with his live-in girlfriend, Melissa, were characterized by the fact that he felt unable to generate much enthusiasm for their relationship, nor indeed for just about anything she seemed to expect of him, which included "*regular*" and meaningful communication and interpersonal attention. He said that he had a tendency to "*withhold*" talking about issues with Melissa, which in turn frustrated her, and that he often forgot to call her when he was supposed to. He also said that he was afraid, since he was still a young man, of being "*screwed by a demanding* relationship" for the rest of his life. Once, while describing his ambivalence about their decision to live together, he said "I wish we at least had separate bathrooms—I mean bedrooms."

Initial Family History

Jim thought of himself as the "shy" child of a "spontaneous" mother, Sandra, and a more distant father, Peter. His parents divorced when Jim was in primary school.

"She's nice," he said of his mother during intake, "very spontaneous. *She's moved a ton*—11 times in 10 years, always looking for a better job in a better town." Jim's relationship with his mother, an enthusiastic "*pot* smoker," seemed to have often put him in the role of an emotional caretaker to her and this position had generalized to other relationships: "In all my relationships throughout time," Jim said, "I feel like people depend on me more than I depend on them." This dynamic, or something like it, seemed to be emerging in his relationship with Melissa as well when I met Jim.

Jim talked less about his father, an emergency medical technician, but described him as "very stable" and quiet, the virtual opposite of his mother. He never remarried, and kept the same job "forever."

Jim stayed in Sandra's custody until his high school years, when he left after months of mounting tension with his mother. She felt that she had lost touch with what Jim was doing, and often criticized him for "not communicating." She began demanding "rap sessions" with him, and taking privileges away if he refused to talk to her. This led to increasingly mean-spirited attacks on Jim's character, often when she was stoned, and finally he left, moving in with his father. In recent years, the relationship had improved, and he came to feel that his mother, who had by then been sober for several years, now treated him respectfully and as a fellow adult.

This synopsis of Jim's clinical picture and family and personal history represent most of what I knew at the beginning of therapy. As in any therapy, what Freud called the "anamnesis" of this patient was less complete in the beginning than at the end of the therapy. My discussion of Jim's case is intended to show that a patient's history (parts of which may have disappeared, much like the "purloined letter") can become more completely articulated via the clinician's (and consequently, the patient's) close attention to the letter of the patient's speech. Here, I will recount one of the many chains of signification that were followed with the result of what Lacan called a "re-membering" of Jim's history.

"I Should Be Punished to Get It through Myself"

> [D]etermining the scope of what discourse repeats … prepares the question of what symptoms repeat.
>
> **—Lacan (1966/2006, p. 13)**

Jim was an extremely "compliant" patient, to borrow a medical term. He showed up consistently and punctually for his sessions, and was receptive to trying his best to free associate when I encouraged him to, even though he sometimes got "*stuck*" (see the text that follows). From the beginning, Jim took up the therapy as a series of themes, which he connected from one session to the next. His earliest topics were related to his ambivalence toward his girlfriend, his career, and about having to speak in psychotherapy. His anxiety about all three of these aspects of his life was bound up in his desire to be "*productive.*" He worried about making the wrong career choices, which would affect his ability to be a productive member of society; he was concerned about failing to maintain a "healthy, productive" relationship with his girlfriend, in which he would give Melissa everything she needed from him; and he felt anxious about being productive for me in psychotherapy by having a lot to say. Consequently, he often found himself "*stuck*" in long silences, especially during the first months of therapy. Yet when he felt stuck, he felt that he should at least come to sit in the therapy room "*for a reasonable amount of time*" to see if he could come up with anything to say. When he did speak at length, he worried that his discourse was not productive in terms of leading to quick and tangible change in his life.

It seemed fairly clear at that point in therapy that Jim's anxiety about being productive enough for Melissa was somehow recapitulative of his need to be productive for his mother. In both cases, he felt a pressure to communicate fully with the woman involved, to attend to her needs and desires, and respond to them with the appropriate behavior. Therefore, at the beginning of the treatment we worked on making some links between his feeling that Melissa needed him to be productive more than he needed her, and his relationship with his "spontaneous" (and emotionally needy) mother.

I approached this work, however, by attending to Jim's *language* rather than its inferred *content*.

For example, Jim described Melissa as "fickle and spontaneous," having made "a bunch of different living and career plans echoing almost word for word an earlier description of his mother. I asked him: "Fickle, spontaneous, a bunch of different living and career plans. Sound familiar?" Jim agreed that it did, and noticed quickly and for the first time the "creepy" similarity between Melissa and his mother. He also noticed that both women had the capacity "*to see the faults and the cracks and holes in me very clearly.*"

The following week, he recounted a conflict he had with Melissa in which he had neglected to call her to finalize plans they had together. While out with his friends, Jim "was very aware" that he was supposed to call her, but "*didn't feel the urgency to do it.* I was just out doing something I was enjoying, and she was just waiting."

I asked Jim if he had any associations to this, and he replied: "It's very similar to what had happened with my mom. One reason for our conflict was that I wouldn't keep her informed when I was out. *I feel like I should be punished to get it through myself* that people care [about] what I'm doing." Finally, Jim told me that he was "glad this happened—I think about fights as a *productive* thing."

I replied, "Hmm … productive?"[2]

"Wait," Jim responded. "So you think that I made this fight happen in order to fulfill my need to be productive? I mean, I think you would think that because they probably teach you that kind of thing *in training.* I perceive myself as someone *in training,* at my job."

Clearly, aspects of Jim's relationship with Melissa hearkened back to that with his mother. Further, both incarnations of this situation pointed to feelings of being "closed-in" with the woman in question and needing to escape. As I touched on in my discussion above, I was actively incorporating these themes into my early work with Jim. But, at the risk of putting too fine a point on things, these are interpretations that rely largely upon what we might call the *content* of Jim's discourse, rather than its *letter.* That is, we see *thematic* similarities between his relationships with

---

[2] I recall that at this moment, I had noticed both Jim's deletion of the word *to* (see below) and his repeated use of the word *productive.* I chose to echo the latter, partially because we were still in the early stages of the treatment and it would be easier to get him to associate to *productive* than to wonder if I was critiquing his grammar or attaching too much importance to a simple mistake.

his girlfriend and mother, which do not depend upon the specific words Jim uses in therapy to point out these themes. Following the letter of his speech, however, we may find another line of possible interpretation that could prove fruitful, one that relates directly to the repetition in Jim's speech of the signifier *productive*.

In the conversation I just related, Jim made a deletion, saying: "I should be punished to get it through myself," which left out part of the more common formulation "get it through *to* myself." I noticed this at the time, and tentatively thought that the idea of "getting something through oneself" seems somewhat suggestive of digestion and excretion. This was by no means an interpretation to which I was attached, nor one that I made aloud, but rather something I decided simply to keep in mind. By entertaining it, however, new light is shed upon Jim's statement that having been punished to get something through himself turned out to be "a *productive* thing"; that is, we might connect punishment with productivity and therefore with excretion.

When I then repeated the word *productive*, Jim replied with his statement that projected upon me the thought that he made the fight happen in order to "fulfill [his] need to be productive," which is informative to our sense of the interpersonal aspect of the therapy, as well as indicative that he thought this himself. Yet the following comment, that I would be inclined to think this as a result of my "training," and that Jim, too, was "*in training*" at his job, takes on new resonance in light of the interpretive hypothesis I proposed above. For when would a person be "punished to get it through himself" if not when he was "in training?"[3]

Without being convinced of the viability of this line of interpretation, I continued through the early part of the therapy to devote part of my attention to listening for signifiers that seemed to fit in with it. I wondered if perhaps Jim's fear of dying in the bathroom had any connection with an early conflict around being productive by way of excretion in the appropriate way and place

[3] Toilet training, that is.

in order to please his mother or some other adult. Jim had stated at the beginning of therapy that his mother had "moved a ton," a phrase that could just as easily apply to a large bowel movement as to a change in residence, and was somewhat "fickle," a near homophone of "fecal." This might also help to explain the preoccupation with productivity with other significant people and issues in his life, including in psychotherapy. One of Jim's early thoughts about psychotherapy was that he needed to work to be productive there, especially for my sake, which may have been an example of transference to me of the motherly role. At the same time, Jim felt that therapy was a privilege: a way of "*pampering [him]self*," which one could read as "putting on Pampers," or diapers, thus giving up the need to excrete where and when an authority figure demanded it.

I can say without exaggeration that this line of thinking struck me at the time as counterintuitive, even absurd. Yet it raises an important question: Upon what do we base our theoretical formulations and therapeutic interventions? What does the patient supply in the session that rises to a level of importance that demands of us a therapeutic response? Are the specific words a patient uses important enough? Indeed, there was no shortage of material accessible via more commonly employed psychodynamic methods, such as the interpretation of the content of Jim's speech, or the interpretation of his affective presentation in light of the therapeutic relationship (he often presented as affectively constricted).

But considered strictly, such methods rely upon impressions that can be substantiated no more concretely than can the interpretation I have offered here. That is, I would have no way of directly witnessing that Jim was using his affective comportment to, say, defend against engaging more fully in the therapeutic relationship. And as Skinner would point out, it is impossible to directly witness that affective flatness itself (a "mentalistic construct," if ever there was one). Yet we may be more accustomed to an intervention based on this kind of inferential assessment, and because we have grown accustomed to such inferences, they may seem more plausible than the strange speculation I introduced previously. However, this more common means of assessment, like the prefect's stubborn belief that the letter must be hidden in some clever contraption, relies upon material that is in no way more readily observable than the material upon which I am basing my interpretive hypothesis (that is, Jim's actual words). What at first glance may seem eminently more sane and simple may in fact be just as (if not more) outlandish and absurd a proposition as the one I have suggested: that we base our assessment upon the letter, and not the inferred intent, of the patient's speech.

In fact, this literal approach, as odd as it may strike us, may involve *less* of a leap of theoretical faith than does the more common approach which takes as its source the inferred content of the patient's speech and behavior. That is, the letter of the patient's speech is *readily observable*. Jim *actually said* the word "productive." This behavior was manifest,[4] and produced an artifact (the word), the nature of which can be verified by any number of independent observers. Although the interpretive speculations I am suggesting rely on what has not been confirmed by the manifest facts, the material I am basing them upon *is* manifest. Hence, we are following Dupin in looking in the most obvious place—the letter of the patient's speech—for the hidden truth we are seeking.

A number of other words, phrases, and slips of the tongue too numerous to catalog here began to appear in Jim's speech which seemed to fit in with the theme of producing versus holding back excreta, but for many weeks there was no stated connection between these two issues. I often simply repeated these words, or perhaps only punctuated them by saying "hmm," or some such ambiguous syllable, wanting only to draw Jim's attention to this

[4] This claim is, of course, subject to numerous objections, not least among them the fact that the listener or reader of any speech is actively co-constructing that which she hears, and it is only via that process that we communicate at all. But I stand by the proposition that words and letters are more readily observable (however subjective our observational capacities are) than invisible, inferred intentions and ideas behind the speech being heard.

part of his discourse, hoping to subtly encourage him to explore it. As I did so, such instances seemed to steadily increase.

During a session about 4 months into the therapy, Jim was speaking about his inability as a child to confront his mother for being "irrational." He complained that when he had opportunities to do so, he simply "got stuck" and "went blank" (an experience that repeated in contemporary relationships as well). I asked him why he would not want to confront his mother. He replied: "wanting to invoid—avoid—the intensity of anger and sadness that I might feel."

While we had spoken at length about Jim's difficulties expressing emotion, I concentrated here upon the slip he had made. Jim responded by associating to the slip, as he had become accustomed by now to my asking him to do so.

"Invoid?" I asked him.

By this time, Jim was learning to free associate, with relatively little direct instruction to do so: "Invoided?" he replied. "Invoked? Invoice, voiding: like pooping or peeing. Silencing my inner voice, voiding into something. Dying, like dying in the bathroom."

The language I had noticed earlier in the therapy *could have* been applicable to matters of the bathroom, and I had some speculations on its connection with Jim's feeling "stuck" and in "a state of arrest" in various places or situations, as well as with his tendency to "withhold" from his mother and girlfriend. But in this conversation, the connection became plain to see, and even somewhat conscious for Jim, even if it was not clear exactly how the connection worked.

"How are you feeling now?" I asked Jim, as I wondered whether this connection brought with it any affect, from which Jim often felt very distanced.

"A little bit sad! Even though we've had conversations about the trouble before with me and my mom, maybe I was sort of caught up in being fine with it. Maybe thinking that was just denying it ever happened in the first place. I'd like to think I've totally forgiven her, but maybe I haven't."

It appeared that having made the new connection between withholding from his mother and going to the bathroom, Jim was now able to lessen his investment in denying how much his mother had hurt him. A relationship he often insisted on characterizing as healthy and egalitarian, with no unresolved conflict now became one in which he might possibly be harboring some resentment, and he was able to articulate something about that resentment. This struck me as therapeutic progress. Yet his words led me to wonder whether they might apply to more than what had happened in Jim's adolescence. After all, the bathroom connection had not yet been thematically explored, and while it was possible that the answer was to be found in Jim's high school years, it seemed more likely that his earlier history was implicated, since control over one's excretion is more often an issue earlier in life. I wondered if there was anything else in this area that he was "caught up in being fine with," and which he was attempting to deny "ever happened in the first place."

To put aside that question momentarily and return to the conversation at hand, Jim later said: "Melissa always wants me to say more."

"Be productive!" I interjected.

"Yeah. My mom wanted me to be productive. *I don't know how to relieve it.*"

"Relieve it?"

"My inner voice. I just learned how to suppress the inner voice until I couldn't hear it anymore."

The "inner voice" that Jim had been speaking about (as a result of exploring his slip, "invoid") was now something that called for *relief*, a word sometimes employed in connection with urination or defecation. Jim learned to "suppress" this inner voice in direct contradiction to the desire of his mother, who wanted him to be more "productive" (perhaps to relieve himself by voiding something). It follows to wonder whether there was some connection between not being productive for his mother by withholding his speech, and not being productive for his mother by withholding feces or urine. To paraphrase his statement, did Jim "learn how to suppress" the need to relieve or void until he couldn't feel it anymore?

Again, even more instances in which Jim's language seemed suggestive of a concern about the withholding and letting go of excreta came up in our sessions, further bolstering the possibility that such an interpretation might have some promise to it, yet I was hesitant to suggest it outright. My hesitation came from several sources: for one, the interpretation seemed quite cliché, as though it belonged in one of those few pages in an introductory psychology textbook that are dedicated to the reduction of Freud to the caricature with whom we are all so familiar. What would my patient, who was very bright, think of such an absurd interpretation? But there was also the issue of technique—of Lacanian technique—which suggested that it may be more fruitful for the patient if I simply punctuated these tropes in his speech, and see how that speech changes over time. Since my project was to attempt a more Lacanian mode of psychotherapy with Jim, I kept myself by and large to this mode of working with him. I encouraged associations, asked open-ended questions, repeated phrases that struck me as particularly ambiguous or polyvalent, and waited to see what would result. By the point in the therapy I am now discussing, Jim had become more "productive" of language that seemed to apply to the bathroom, and (as we just saw) began to make some conscious connections between productivity and going to the bathroom. Therefore, I chose not to act too quickly by making an interpretation about the possible events of early childhood toilet training. Rather, I decided to continue as I had been working, in the hope that Jim could make interpretations or historical connections himself, which I believe to be more valuable than his simply taking the word of his therapist.

The Productive Letter

After about 7 months of weekly sessions involving this approach to this particular material, Jim was again discussing his tendency to "hold back" from his girlfriend emotionally, verbally, and behaviorally. Jim noted: "I do hold myself off from getting too invested in the relationship."

"Hold myself off ..." I echoed.

"I'm wondering what you meant by repeating that," Jim mused. I find that patients have varying degrees of tolerance for frequent repetitions of their own words, but Jim tended to find them interesting. "Restricting myself from doing things. Silencing myself. This line of thinking makes sense. I feel like over the last two sessions, I thought more about who I was as a child. I was an internalizer, shy, quiet, unexpressive, timid, even along the lines of bodily functions. *I had a serious problem with constipation when I was younger.* I could be internalizing in my life right now. I probably am. It makes sense that I could be holding myself off from feeling."

To my surprise, Jim had confirmed the hypothesis I had been entertaining for several months. Not only did he state that he had had a "serious problem with constipation," but he connected this to his lack of emotional and vocal "productivity" as well. I asked him more about the issue:

"What else do you remember about the constipation?"

"It was in, maybe fourth grade. I was constipated a lot, and my mom was really worried. She took me to the doctor's. He bent me over in front of my mother and examined me. He made me use suppositories and, like, gave me one in front of her. It was pretty big-time. There was no physical cause. ... My mom would ask me if I had to go to the bathroom, and if I said no, she'd tell me to try anyway. I guess I felt forced by her to stay in the bathroom for *a certain amount of time*. ... It was like I had to keep myself in the bathroom *as long as I felt was reasonable*."

A possible objection to placing any importance upon this memory may be that constipation can be viewed as simply a physical problem, which need not take on any special meaning. As I mentioned above, it can seem a bit cliché in this post-Freudian age to make the case that it does. Yet the fact that Jim brought up this memory at all indicates that it must have some importance *for him*; that it was more than just some incidental physical problem. Further, Jim stated that "there was no physical cause" of the constipation itself, indicating the possibility that it was a psychogenic symptom, thus making it all the more deserving of careful attention. Finally, and perhaps most importantly, *Jim himself made the connection* between his interpersonal functioning, his emotional life, and his history of constipation. I never made the interpretation.

Here again we see Jim's mother intimately involved with his need to be productive. It was her concern over Jim's lack of productivity that led her to take him to the doctor's office. Jim's experience of the doctor's examination and administration of the first suppository was traumatic. So it turned out that Jim's earlier statement, "I feel like I should be punished to get it through myself," a slip that may appear extremely unimportant, like the letter laying upon the desk of the minister in Poe's story, turned out to be vitally important to Jim's history. Because he failed to "get it through himself," he had been punished with a highly unpleasant medical procedure. The reader will recall that after Jim mentioned this feeling that he should be punished, he stated that that kind of punishment (in that instance, the fight with Melissa) was "a *productive* thing." Again, if the medical treatment was his punishment, this was applicable, since shortly after the procedure, Jim defecated. Hence, both in his fight with Melissa and his struggle over the control of his body with his mother, being "punished to get it through [him]self" was a "productive thing."

The polyvalence of another phrase of Jim's also bears mentioning here. Jim had mentioned (see previous text) that both his mother and his girlfriend could "see his faults and cracks and holes clearly." If his lack of verbal and behavioral productivity was taken to be a fault of his that they both saw clearly (which it was), and we connect that lack of productivity to his lack of productivity of feces at a young age (which he did), then we might see the medical procedure as an excellent example of his mother's invasiveness, who of course accompanied him, and saw his "faults and cracks and holes" quite clearly, as the doctor exposed Jim in front of her.

But there was more to the punishment than one medical intervention. As a follow-up treatment to the procedure, Jim was given suppositories, which his mother administered to him, to alleviate the problem. Further, he was "forced by her to stay in the bathroom for a certain amount of time" even when he did not feel that he had to go to the bathroom. On several occasions, after he refused to go to the bathroom, his mother would spank him, another quite literal punishment. Therefore, if Jim was not productive for his mother, he risked being spanked, anally penetrated, forced to stay in the bathroom for a "reasonable" length of time, or being taken to the doctor to endure more unpleasant procedures, by which his mother could see his faults, cracks, and holes clearly. (It may warrant pointing out again that early in the therapy with *this* doctor, when Jim was "stuck" for something to say, he felt that he should sit in the therapy room "for a reasonable amount of time" as well).

THE VALUE OF THE LETTER IN THE GREATER THERAPEUTIC CONTEXT

Arguably, there was some potential connection between Jim's preoccupation with being productive, his fear of being locked in bathrooms, and these childhood memories. Indeed, Jim found a great many such connections in the course of his therapy, a number of which functioned on the same linguistic principles I am discussing here.

It is the aim of this chapter, however, neither to fully formulate the way in which these elements functioned together, nor to give a complete exposition of Jim's therapy, nor even to report therapeutic outcomes. Rather, my aim here is simply to preliminarily illustrate the way in which close attention to the letter of the patient's speech can yield material and insights that are therapeutically relevant and potentially powerful, while more complete clinical expositions are given in the following cases. In Jim's case, the letter of his speech was indicative of an important memory, one that provided a central metaphor for his current problems. That memory finally came into Jim's manifest discourse after the parts of his speech that indicated it were consistently and noninvasively punctuated for several months. That memory, in turn, furnished a major turning point in his therapy, a place from which to build new insights, to reexamine memories and habits of intrapsychic and interpersonal functioning, and to begin to feel "competent as an adult," which had been his original goal.

Various dynamic therapies have various ways of setting about these goals, and what I am calling "following the letter" is but one among many. As this chapter illustrates, however, this technique is remarkable inasmuch as it relies upon material that is far from hidden in the "black box" of the unconscious. Noticing the specifics of Jim's speech did not require any privileged information about what he was "really" thinking or feeling; rather, it required only that I be attuned to the peculiarities of his words. To be sure, I did make hypotheses about what these letters might have been indicating, but I made them silently. The technique of punctuation (pointing out peculiarities of speech that I noticed by raising my eyebrows, saying "hmm," repeating Jim's words, etc.) allowed me not to make premature interpretations, instead *letting the material come from Jim when he was ready*—perhaps an experience that this patient found novel.

In Poe's "The Purloined Letter," Dupin carries out his search not by probing for secret compartments that may have been created inside of furniture or walls, but by looking first in the patently, ridiculously obvious place. We can be sure that the prefect of police would have scoffed at such an exercise, perhaps from more than a little fear that he might look downright silly if he were to engage in it. Lacan (2006) might be warning the clinician not to fall into the trap that snares the prefect, whose knowledge of secret compartments is so impressive that he is unable to find the hidden item. Instead, perhaps we should not to be too afraid to look in a place that is so patently obvious, so accessible, that we feel slightly embarrassed even to look there for the unconscious clinical material we are seeking.

Of course, the goal of following the letter is not simply to find out what it says. It doesn't particularly matter in and of itself that Jim was constipated as a child. Rather, the goal of finding the letter is to free it to become once again a part of the patient's discourse, a discourse that has as its potential the psychological growth that psychoanalytic therapies make it their business to promote. As long as the signifier remains *en souffrance*, however, our patients may continue to suffer as well.

This case study is not focused on outcomes, nor does it in any way attempt an exhaustive account of Jim's therapy, which I believe was rich with examples of the benefit of following the letter. But it seems worth mentioning that Jim's therapy ended with him in a remarkably different place from where he began, despite the fact that the termination was due to circumstances beyond our control. Jim left therapy having also ended the romantic relationship he was "stuck" in when he began, having made a major and successful change in his career, and, perhaps most importantly, having begun to seek a deeper emotional and communicative connection with his distant father; a desire for this last element was ultimately implied in much of Jim's symbolic material (a heart attack implies the need for an EMT, after all) and finally owned by Jim.

POWER AND THERAPY

The question must arise: What were the interventions I've described here like for Jim? As with each of the case studies I present in this book, what I have described here comes to the reader lacking much of the context in which it originally took place. I bring this up here because Jim's experience of these interventions (and my decisions to make them) took place within a setting of what I perceived to be a strong therapeutic relationship, in which

I took pains to co-create an environment with Jim where he felt as safe as possible to pursue his therapeutic work, where he felt taken seriously yet not pathologized, and where he felt that I was working from a perspective of basic respect and care. Because the centrality of the basic therapeutic relationship is not the focus of this book, it is easy for the interventions I am describing here to appear stranger and colder than they in fact felt at the time. I ask the reader to hold in mind that everything I present in these case studies took place within the larger context of a basically good working alliance.

Hence, when we ask what the above moments in therapy were like for Jim, we must keep in mind this background of relationship. But this caveat does not at all immunize these interventions from some theoretical and ethical inconsistencies. In fact, it may serve to make one objection even stronger. That objection is as follows.

One strength that I have claimed for the theory and technique I have presented in this chapter is the lengths to which Lacan seems to go in his attempts not to remake the patient's ego in the shape of the clinician's (see Chapter 1). I have held to the idea that a basic respect for the patient's subjectivity is one of the engines of Lacanian theory. It cannot be avoided, however, that my punctuations of Jim's language, for example, were chosen according *my own* subjectivity. I could not have followed the letter of all of Jim's language and still have done any meaningful work, and I therefore was selective in what I attended to—in the parts of therapy I have presented here, what I attended to was language that seemed to refer to excretion. It is true that I attempted to limit my repetitions of words, and my verbal and nonverbal punctuations of various signifiers, to that which struck me as particularly polyvalent, or to that which seemed to appear with unusual frequency in Jim's language. Yet it would be absurd to try to make the case that my decisions to highlight some words and not others was determined only by objective factors rather than being influenced by my own receptivity to some elements over others.

If I was intervening based at least partially upon my own predispositions and subjective impressions, then the question must be asked: How is the clinician to do this ethically? Renik (1999) might suggest that we "play our cards face up" in psychotherapy and disclose to the patient the reasons we are interested in a particular turn of phrase or idea, thus owning our half of the exchange and preventing the patient from having to fulfill a function as our narcissistic extension (or alter-ego), a possibility that Lacan, too, seems to want to prevent from fruition. In the interventions I have described here, I generally did not disclose my reasons for action, or my interest in the particular signifiers I picked up on, or even the purpose of the interventions themselves. That is, in our already existent relationship, Jim could afford to see my raised eyebrows at a particular time as being nothing special, just a sign of my interest. Yet I was acting very purposefully at such times, carefully choosing the words after which I subtly intervened. Such actions were designed to encourage Jim to speak more along the lines of the signifiers to which I had reacted, thus opening up more discourse around what I saw as a pivotal issue. The case can be made that I was engaged in basic Skinnerian shaping.

The ethical problem that arises here is this: How can I claim to be respecting the patient's subjectivity when I am arguably subtly manipulating him into associating to ideas which I, and not he, have deemed to be important? Asking whether the intervention accomplishes its goal leaves out the question of whether it violates the patient in any way. Asking how comfortable Jim was during the process may not be the right question either, since it is fairly easy to make a person comfortable before violating him, but this does not change the fact that he is violated.

There are probably several ways to answer this charge, but I do not claim that any of them is entirely satisfactory. We can say, for example, that the clinician is supposed to be well-enough aware of his own psychology to be reasonably able to prevent an abuse of the power he has over the patient in this context, but such a claim is far from demonstrated in the field of psychotherapy, if it is indeed demonstrable at all. We can say, with Lacan, that it is more a disservice to the patient to explain one's own agenda at all times than not to, since the former makes the healing, enigmatic desire of the analyst for the subject to speak into a concrete demand that the patient can then easily fulfill or frustrate, thereby becoming either a carbon copy or a negative image of the analyst's ego. Then again, the difference may only be the degree of subtlety of manipulation. As with any therapy, a meaningful struggle with the issues of power and the therapeutic relationship as they are implicated in an implementation of Lacanian theory is something that should never be far from our practice. I cannot say that I have been satisfied with any particular answer to this problem, and much of what is presented here lends itself to this kind of debate.[5]

LACAN AND EXISTENTIALISM

Although there is much of theoretical interest in Lacan's "Seminar on 'The Purloined Letter,'" and much from which complex theoretical elaborations can be and have been constructed, I have attempted in this chapter to highlight what I believe is an appeal to simplicity that lies at the heart of that essay: the injunction to notice what is obviously there. And while Lacan's treatment of "The Purloined Letter" has been discussed by a number of other authors (see, for example, Fink, 1995; Felman, 1988), I have tried here to bring the essay in question into close dialogue with clinical concerns.

The first of these points helps this chapter to lay the groundwork for an ostensibly unlikely alliance between Lacanian thinking and other, more pragmatic perspectives. My interpretation of Lacan's writing—as advocating attention to that which we can readily see and hear (the letter of patient's language), and to explore the multiple possibilities of meaning that flow from these readily

[5] Yet I might also point out that while a Lacanian approach does not seem to entirely solve this problem, it is hardly unique in struggling with it. Every psychotherapist, in the end, intervenes based upon his own subjectivity and theoretical perspective.

observable phenomena—contains within it invitations to several other psychological disciplines. Among these is the tradition of existential phenomenology as articulated by Heidegger (an acquaintance of Lacan) in the discipline of philosophy, and Boss within psychology, and elaborated upon by van den Berg, Sartre, R. D. Laing, and others. An objection brought by the existential phenomenologists to psychoanalysis and Hegelian philosophy is the utter lack of a reference point in the lived world for some of the constructs that these modes of thinking seem to force upon their subject matter. And, as the reader may be aware, Lacan himself (e.g., 1949/2002) was harshly critical of the existential approach to psychology with its tenet that the person can be self-transparent.

But Lacan's work, I propose, offers a mode of hearing that stays quite grounded in what is demonstrable and pursues a kind of phenomenology of the letter to psychotherapeutic ends.

4

Aggressiveness in Psychotherapy

> [R]eading in no way obliges you to understand. You have to read first.
>
> **—Lacan (1975, p. 65)**

> The unconscious is what is read.
>
> **—Lacan (1975, p. 26)**

THE LETTER AND THE TRANSFERENCE

We may (or may not) be impressed by case formulations that focus on language as their primary point of reference, and may (or may not) be drawn into the game of following odd linguistic connections in the patient's narrative, even if only for the sheer intellectual fun that it can bring. But after reading the previous chapter, clinicians may make the objection that it is hard to imagine Lacan and his "linguistricks" having much of value to offer the practitioner in the here-and-now of the therapeutic *relationship*. Many therapists who consider themselves strongly psychodynamic and psychoanalytic in their orientation attend closely and thematically to the relationship and its consequent transference and countertransference, and rely upon interpretations of one or the other (usually the former, but in recent years the latter has come to prominence) as a major component of the therapy. The attention paid in this area is generally more concerned with dynamics of feeling and nonverbal behavior between therapist and patient than it is with attention to the letter of the patient's language as I am approaching it in this book.

This chapter will attempt to illustrate how a Lacanian approach to psychotherapy might listen to the transference as it announces itself in the peculiarities of the patient's language. I will also discuss one possible approach taken on the basis of this kind of listening to a patient whose language bespeaks some contempt or aggressiveness toward the therapist, integrating a discussion of Lacan's early paper "Aggressiveness in Psychoanalysis" (1948/2002). In other words, my guiding question throughout the case study that follows is this: How might the clinical discipline of "following the letter" impact a therapist's approach to negative transference?

THE CASE OF ERIC

Presenting Information

Eric Borta was 47 years old when I met him. He was originally referred to me as a result of his then-therapist having to take unexpected time away from her practice. We met for about 16 months.

Eric first came to my office unsure of what had become of his previous therapist. He presented as generally well-defended and justifiably wary of his new circumstances. Attempting to discern his therapeutic goals, problems, and general experience, I felt that I was learning very little, and continued to press for something like a presenting problem. But over and over, my feeling was that Eric's difficulty was precisely his *lack* of a presenting problem, or at least one that he seemed clear about.

Eric told me he had been working on "self-esteem" issues up to now that tied in with his being "depressed." Eric considered himself a writer, and had written a number of short stories, but his passion was for acting. Eric's abiding interest in acting began in early childhood with a fascination with movies, and eventually led him to seek out acting work in California as a young man—an adventure that Eric felt was curtailed prematurely. Like his more recent hesitation to get involved again in acting or attempt to publish his stories, many of Eric's complaints involved a feeling of malaise, a vague desire to be somewhere else, or some*thing* else, but a lack of motivation to get there.

Perhaps the most striking example of this was Eric's living situation. He lived with, and in fact still shared a bed with, his ex-wife. Their relationship had begun more than 15 years prior to my meeting Eric, but its romantic phase had lasted only about 10 years. For the last 5 years, Eric and Elaine had continued living together in Elaine's house, sleeping in the same bed even while they (more often Elaine) pursued other relationships. Currently, Elaine was in a long-term relationship with another man, but hid from her new boyfriend the fact that she and Eric still shared such close quarters. Eric was single, dating only occasionally.

What kept Eric living there, as he saw it, were two dogs, three cats, saltwater aquarium fish, a parrot, and five chickens. Leaving the house would mean leaving his animals. He saw himself as the primary caretaker of these animals, and that role was not something he would easily give up. "I like to take care of things that can't protect themselves," he told me. His pets were one example of this predilection: Each of them had been "unwanted" when he took it in.

His animals were not the only parties in the house that Eric saw as needing his care. His ex-wife had been suffering with a rare heart problem for years, having been first diagnosed shortly before their relationship began. Elaine told him about her condition when they first began dating, and Eric decided that his role would now involve taking care of a chronically and severely ill woman. But Elaine, with proper medical care, continued to lead an active life despite her condition. Nevertheless, Eric had come to settle into the role of caretaker over time. When I met him years later, he was still cleaning and running the household, while his wife enjoyed a full social life and daily trips to the gym.

Despite his long-held ambition to become an actor, Eric had remained all these years in an entry-level retail position. He disliked his job, disliked the pay, and frequently thought of leaving for the West Coast to pursue his dream. Yet he kept at it, always invoking the same reason: He was needed at home.

In so many aspects of his life, Eric was going through the motions—emotionally distanced and divested from his routine, yet somehow unable to give it up. His attitude toward psychotherapy (prior to our working together) seemed much the same: He had been showing up once a month, but didn't seem quite sure why he had come in the first place, nor by that same token whether anything had improved for him.

I suggested to Eric during our first meeting that we meet weekly rather than monthly. I explained to him that I would be able to make little clinical difference for him if we only met monthly, especially since I had such a vague idea of his presenting problems and history. I offered him a trial period of 1 month of weekly sessions, which would give both of us a better idea how therapy might go, and he agreed.

Then Eric said mockingly, as if in my voice: "Oh good! I can get paid now!" It would seem that he had found someone else who needed his help.

This was the first of a number of comments, actions, and jokes, particularly common during the first weeks of therapy, which seemed to express some contempt for me. In this chapter I will discuss this early phase of therapy, in which Eric's transference seemed particularly aggressive.

History and Family Dynamics

Eric was the second of two children, having been born about 8 years after his sister Edie. He was the unplanned child of a father, Jack, whose success as a surgeon, and narcissistic investment therein, kept him noticeably more involved in his work than in his family life. He therefore tended to see his father as a marginal presence at best, and although he feared his father's occasional outbursts over messes and noise in the house, it was hard to see any evidence that Eric had much respect for him. Eric's mother Edna, on the other hand, was accorded more of what a social psychologist might see as a mixture of coercive and referent power over him—the ability to induce Eric to please her, as well as the ability to hurt him deeply—and this resulted in much of Eric's life being subsequently organized around trying to accomplish the former. Early on, when I asked Eric about his previous experiences in therapy, he related the story of a drawing he had made for art class as a kindergartener. The assignment was to draw his family. Eric produced a drawing of his mother inside a movie theater, his father in a hospital, and Eric in the house.

His mother was often at the movies, leaving Eric with his older sister. It may be no coincidence that, in the ensuing years, Eric became fascinated with movies, fantasizing often about being on the screen that had his mother's attention. In fact, Eric's goal years later as he graduated high school was to become a famous actor. He even moved to Los Angeles in order to try to make his way in the industry, and once there, began to make professional connections. In fact, Eric had just received a casting callback for a high-profile commercial after several months of struggling, when his mother called. When he gave her the news of his job prospect, she told him that it was "cute" that he was doing this, but that he would probably never make it as an actor anyhow, given his lack of talent. The speech deflated Eric's self-esteem enough that he slept through the callback the next morning. Having missed his chance for the job, he decided to return home for the summer. There, he met Elaine, and never returned to California.

Edna was a much-feared disciplinarian, with most of Eric's memories of parental discipline involving her and not his father. Memories of his mother beating him with a stick, or telling him to "go get the belt" for beatings, and locking him in his bedroom were among the examples. Eric did his best to conform to his mother's expectations of him, and stayed away from smoking, drinking, and any kind of recreational drug use, on into his adult life: "I never did anything Mom would be ashamed of."

Eric also characterized his relationship with his mother as marked by mistrust. Two stories are illustrative.

About midway through his high school years, Eric's sister Edie gave birth to a little girl, and moved back in with the family to care for her. At this time, the family (who lived in a rural area) owned several chickens, one of which Eric considered to be his own, and cared for regularly in its backyard coop. The night Eric's niece came home from the hospital, the family celebrated with a chicken dinner, courtesy of Eric's pet. No one had warned him about this, and he learned of his friend's demise when remarking on how good the chicken was. He remembered his mother laughing as she told him where, or whom, it had come from.

Shortly afterward, Eric became a vegetarian. He recalled that his mother, who was aware of his new diet, made a casserole one day, and upon his asking, told him that the dish was entirely vegetarian, containing cubed tofu. When he took a bite, it was clear that he was eating chicken. His mother replied to his confrontation with a blasé, "Oh, you noticed?"

Early Course of the Transference: The Man Who Worked for Apple

As I've mentioned, Eric began treatment wary of his new circumstances and appeared defensive toward the idea of taking up a position of any vulnerability in therapy. He often made hostile jokes about what I must be thinking during the first two sessions, and outside of that said very little, especially about himself. Eric seemed not to be engaging in therapy at all, but instead, biding his time. I began to wonder, even by the second session, what Eric was doing there at all. He appeared at times to want no help, indeed to have no presenting problem at all other than his reported "low self-esteem," the meaning of which he doggedly refused to shed any light on. He also seemed to take great pleasure in insulting me for being a young, student therapist. Yet he was showing up, and had in fact agreed to increase his frequency of treatment to once per week. He must have wanted something.

This brings us to the difficulty of how to approach the transference. Lacan is noted for his admonitions not to interpret the transference to the patient, and Fink (2004) provides a helpful synopsis of the reasons why: "Whenever analysts are inclined to interpret 'the transference,' they are likely to be interpreting the imaginary component alone and not the overall symbolic framework" (p. 19). In the following text, I will attempt to explore what it might mean to resist the urge to interpret in the imaginary register and opt instead to open up the realm of the symbolic by means of following the patient's language "to the letter."

During the second session, I decided that simply containing Eric's apparent hostility was not enough, and that doing so in a more or less passive manner, although perhaps helping to "hold" him in therapy, á la Winnicott (1986), would perhaps only have the counterproductive effect of holding him back from engagement with the psychological material. I therefore made an early interpretive move that I felt might bring us into a more productive mode of discourse. I asked Eric whether his hostile jokes (which he readily recognized as such) might have a function. Eric countered that he didn't understand my question, so (responding to the demand inherent in his reply) I offered that perhaps his jokes and his silence help protect him from "something in the therapeutic project" that made him uncomfortable.

Given the premise that the therapist is to resort to interpretations (especially so early in the treatment) only sparingly, inasmuch as they tend to place the therapist–patient relationship more firmly on the imaginary axis (this intervention, for example, can be seen as my saying: "*I* want you to stop acting that way, and start acting this way"), there seems to be nothing particularly Lacanian about my move here. On the other hand, if we reexamine the dynamic during the first two sessions, we find a situation in which (a) speech is impoverished (Eric refused to speak much), and (b) competition for dominance begins to become a salient theme. Eric may have been keeping himself in the dominant position by neutralizing me and my supposed thoughts (which were, of course, his own thoughts projected onto the person of the therapist, that is, the thoughts of the Other) via his mocking narrations of what I might be thinking. Further, through his silence, he may have been making an attempt to arouse and frustrate my desire (the desire of the analyst/therapist) (Lacan, 1960/2002; Fink, 1997) for him to speak, thus keeping me in a position of supplication rather than the (threatening) position of the subject-supposed-to-know. In any case, discourse had stopped almost before it had begun, and had been replaced by a sort of uneasy, silent staring contest.

By making this semi-interpretive move, I was attempting to invite Eric out of the immobility of the imaginary register and into a stance from which he could begin to understand the symbolic value held by his silence and sarcastic remarks. I did not name what he might be protecting himself from, but instead offered an open-ended question about whether his behavior might be doing *something* to protect himself from *something*. Certainly I may have said a bit too much here for the demands of the approach in question. It would perhaps have been better not to satisfy his demand by explaining more clearly what I meant by my question. But at the same time, I had a therapeutic alliance to build, which is a necessity I don't believe Lacanian therapy is (or should be) exempt from. We are *always* to some extent tied to the imaginary axis in our relations with our therapists and patients, and the relationship must necessarily exploit this to some extent, especially toward the beginning of therapy.

The intervention seemed to prove fruitful. The third session began with Eric stating: "I think I have an issue about having a male therapist. But it might be good for me." I inquired as to what the issue might be, and Eric answered that he was afraid of "repeating a pattern of relationships that didn't work out." Later in the session, he mentioned feeling "threatened, defensive, and angry" because of the difference in our respective ages.

"It's like someone younger than me doing something better than I do. I feel trapped."

"Trapped?" I punctuated the word.

"Yeah. Like with children. And abortion.[1] Parents feel trapped by children."

"Abortion."

Eric clarified that parents feeling trapped might lead them to abort their pregnancies. Later in the session, Eric mentioned that one of his short stories featured a self-administered abortion, in which a pregnant woman attempted to destroy the "devil seed" she was carrying.

Eric also delved into his thoughts about therapy itself: his expectations and fantasies about what might happen. He expressed a wish to be "hypnotized" in order to find out about mistakes he made in his "past life." Noticing the ambiguity in the phrase "past life," which could be taken as referring to past incarnations or simply to the part of his current life that has passed, I simply echoed that phrase: "past life." He responded, "Yeah. Are there thoughts in my head I don't know about?" and gave the example of repressed sexual abuse in childhood. Eric went on to describe "a void" he sensed in his mind and memory, a "black spot" where something may have been blocked out. Through hypnosis, he wanted me to "reach in and pull something out of [him]" (another phrase with strong overtones of pregnancy).

This apparent preoccupation—conscious and unconscious—with pregnancy, childbirth, children, and abortion showed up again in a number of subsequent sessions. Eric began the fourth session (for which he arrived several minutes late) by expressing his annoyance with parents who pick up their children at school, thus congesting traffic and making him late, and threw in for good measure that most of these children would have their education wasted on them.

---

[1] Note Eric's last name, Borta.

He also mentioned a dream, stating simply that it had been about: "a guy I see at Starbuck's who thinks I like them but I didn't like." I asked Eric to elaborate.

"When I go on my break from work to Starbucks I always see this guy, the manager at the Apple Store. He brings people there for meetings, comes in for business. I always notice he doesn't tip very well. Sometimes he starts talking with me about the crossword puzzle or whatever, and he's always asking about my personal life. I ignored him [in the dream] and walked away from him."

"Anything come to mind about Apple?"

"Jealousy. I see their employees sitting at Starbucks. And iPods, and apple, a fruit. Bearing fruit. Something you eat, or don't like. A pregnant belly."

In such cases, I did not interpret. I hadn't gathered enough information to make a case formulation cogent enough for interpretation. Nor had we developed a strong enough alliance within those first 4 weeks; less than one month into the therapy, an interpretation of the material *per se* might only serve to stifle the rich stream of material that Eric had only just begun to produce. Instead, I pursued his associations, and timed my own ambiguous reactions, such as raising my eyebrows, or saying "aha" or "mm hmm" to encourage him to pursue this imagery of pregnancy (and, at times, its termination). The "analyst's desire" was being engaged now: Eric was speaking.

Despite my decision not to make interpretations to Eric, I began to see themes emerging. Certainly there was, up to now, a motif involving pregnancy and abortion. If, as he had already stated, I was the party he expected to reach in and pull something out of him (as a midwife or obstetrician would), might I be somehow implicated in this dream as the *man who works for apple* (an apple being that disliked fruit with which Eric was pregnant)? Like the man in the dream, I was indeed there for business ("comes in for business"). Eric had also found my lack of direction frustrating ("doesn't tip very well"). And we had already discussed his *jealousy* of me. I was also "always asking about [Eric's] personal life."

Furthermore, during the last two sessions Eric had begun to speak more freely in therapy, moving from open hostility toward therapy to compliance with my expectations, and it would make sense for Eric to surmise that this favor he was doing for me—just as he humored the man from Apple—made me feel that he liked me.

But perhaps the dream tells us I was laboring[2] under the illusion that Eric liked me a bit more than he in fact did! This fantasy might regain for Eric the power he had recently relinquished in therapy.

It appeared obvious that Eric felt hesitation about therapy, and even some hostility toward me; one hardly need turn to Lacanian theory to come away with that information. What is useful about this kind of speculation, though, is that it tells the clinician something about what underlies that hostility and the connections it has with Eric's psychological situation more generally. Eric is casting himself, if my interpretation is correct, as pregnant with that which I don't have, that which I want, and threatens me with not producing it via his allusions to abortion. He can be taken to be saying, "I won't give you the baby you want, no matter how hard you work for it." Not only will he withhold this baby, but true to the name he was given, he'll "abort" it if I make him feel too "trapped." As he identifies, therefore, with his mother (as phallically pregnant) he invokes the power of his father's name to frustrate my supposed desire.

The Developing Transference: A Serious Dogfight

> We must, nevertheless, bring out the subject's aggressiveness toward us, because, as we know, aggressive intentions form the negative transference that is the inaugural knot of the analytic drama.
>
> **—Lacan (1948/2002, p. 16)**

Increasingly, Eric seemed to have taken to simply reporting dreams, associating very little to them, and not engaging in much conversation about them, thus technically satisfying one of the demands of the therapy (talking about dreams) while still frustrating my desire that he say everything that comes to mind. In

[2] Pun intended.

line with my brief previous discussion of the theme of pregnancy and abortion, it seemed to me as though Eric was testing my abilities as a therapist to "pull something out" of him via a mystical reading of his dreams. This afforded him the opportunity to remain aloof from the therapy (as in the dream of 2 weeks prior he "ignored [me] and walked away"). Toward the end of one such session, I made a process comment to the effect that his reticence to engage with the material he brought to therapy was striking.

Upon arriving 15 minutes late for the following appointment (which seemed a fairly sure sign of his irritation with my previous comment), Eric began by saying, "something you said to me last week started to upset me, but I don't remember what it was."

"Hmm," I replied. Rather than making an interpretation about the evident resistance, or the connection between whatever had upset him and his lateness, I threw him a curveball by asking, "Would forgetting it accomplish something?"

Strangely, Eric didn't skip a beat. While my question didn't seem to surprise him, it did yield some fast and unexpected associations. "Like at work, like letting things go that other people do when they mess up or something. Or letting go of when Elaine says I'm doing a bad job with the dogs—"

"Mmm?"

"Anyway, I had another dream."

It seemed likely that Eric had been disturbed by my pointing out his reticence to discuss dreams and other material the previous week—I had stood in the way of the wish that his recent dream of the "man who worked for Apple/apple" had sought to satisfy. That is, I refused to be satisfied with his ruse of allowing me to think he was engaged in the therapy, or with his quick dream reports, for example. Again, I made no suggestion of this theory, but instead decided to punctuate the word "dogs" since they seemed tied up with Eric's notion of unwanted babies,[3] which in turn tied into his

[3] The reader will recall that his animals were "unwanted" when he took them in. At other times, he referred to them as his "babies."

discourse about therapy, as discussed above. This may have been fortuitous, as his subject-change to his dream occurred here, and as we will see, this dream too tied in with his dogs.

"I was in some locker room. There were people around. I don't remember if they were adults or children. I went to the bathroom. In a republic[4]—public bathroom—"

"Uh huh ..."

"—Or locker room–type setting. I don't like that. I like my private space. I was relieving myself in a drawer in this locker room. Someone says 'you're not supposed to do that in there. Wake up.' It was a locker room, I think, but a desire[5]—designer locker room."

"Mm hmm ..."

"The drawer was really white. Everything was clean. I couldn't see anything, but I knew people were there. There was tile on the wall."

"So, the drawer ..."

"Empty. It didn't have a handle on it. It was Formica."

"Formica."

"It was bright. Reflection. A glare from it being so white and clean."

"Mm hmm ..."

"Me soiling it. Making it dirty, oily."

"Dirty and oily? Does that bring anything to mind?"

"Dogs. My little dog and my bigger dog. The little one scares the bigger dog. So the big dog wets the floor. I don't like it at all! It may escalate into a serious dogfight."

"Ah. A serious dogfight!"

"But so far, it's just playful. The big dog does tease him, so they *can* interact."

Unfortunately, there was not time during this session (having lost 15 minutes, we had only half an hour to work) to get

---

[4] Eric's mother was a republican, and politics were a point of contention between them, as Eric was a member of the socialist party.

[5] See previous section for a discussion of the place desire is taking in the therapeutic relationship at this point in the treatment. This is just one aspect of his narration of the dream that makes the "desire locker room" look remarkably like my office.

anywhere near the number of associations that I might have preferred. However, as the dialogue shows, there were several images and associations of note.

To begin with, we have Eric "relieving" himself into a "drawer" in a locker room or public bathroom. He has lost his "private space," and is surrounded by people whom he cannot tell are adults or children. This is a strikingly similar situation to that of his new therapy, where he feels ambivalent about *revealing* (a phonic anagram of "relieving")[6] himself to a younger person who is in a position of power and authority (me), and thus seems both older and younger than Eric at the same time ("I don't remember if they were adults or children").

The drawer in which he relieves/reveals himself is white and reflective, an apt metaphor for the quasi "blank-screen" approach I took to his therapy, in which I did not reveal details about my person, but instead focused upon reflecting the discourse of the patient.[7] At the same time, the drawer was "Formica." Eric called me Michael, and it requires only a slight alteration to read his narration this way: "I was relieving/revealing myself in a drawer *for Michael*."

Finally, we might ask ourselves why the dreamer chose a "drawer" in the first place. In following the letter, we find in the choice of "drawer" a word that yields "reward" when reversed.

Thus, using these alternate readings of Eric's dream, we can track an alternate construction of the dream as follows:

"I *relieved* myself in a Formica drawer."

---

[6] Certainly, he is also "revealing" himself in the dream inasmuch as it is necessary to "expose" himself in order to urinate.

[7] I am not suggesting that the classical notion of the "blank screen" is one that holds up to much philosophical scrutiny. It has been sufficiently demonstrated in any number of places that we are always revealing—to use the word of the moment here—aspects of ourselves intentionally or not, and that our interactions with others occur at levels beyond our conscious control. However, the difference here is that, rather than taking this fact as a reason to be more disclosive generally (a la Renik), I continued to be quite guarded about how much of myself (my "ego") I revealed to Eric, in keeping with the Lacanian notion of eschewing the imaginary in favor of the symbolic.

"I *revealed* myself in a *Formica* drawer."
"I revealed myself in a *drawer for Michael.*"
"I revealed myself as a *reward* for Michael."

Although one facet of this dream text suggests vulnerability (relieving/revealing), if we keep in mind the dog association[8] we can also find an overtone of *aggressiveness* here. Eric is, perhaps, marking his territory and leaving me the resultant gift ("for Michael").[9]

Like the "little dog" at home, I had made Eric uncomfortable by virtue of my position as therapist combined with my age, and he responded not only by becoming frightened (fear of the little dog induces the big dog to urinate on the floor) and relieving himself in the drawer, but also by *marking his own territory.* In allowing this, the dream ensures that Eric will not be annihilated by the children/adults/little dogs/therapist that surround him. After all, he doesn't stop when they tell him to.

Hence, although therapy and the therapist were still threatening to Eric, and he may not have been able to abide the kind of "reflection"[10] I desired from him—in fact, "it may escalate into a serious dogfight"—Eric was still able to "tease" me, thus remaining somewhat aggressive—relieving himself at the same time as he revealed himself—and thereby ensure that we "*can* interact."

---

[8] The reader will recall that Eric brought up this dream at the moment when I had punctuated the word "dog" earlier in the session.

[9] If we take this in the context of the discussion of pregnancy, we might note the way in which, not unlike childbirth, Eric produces something from his genital region for the therapist. But it is perhaps not without importance that this time, my reward is not a baby at all—it is urine, and comes not from a vagina but from a penis. One alternate reading of the dream is that it declares, "I won't give you the baby I know you want. I'll piss on you instead. You want me to be a woman, but I will be a man." This is further corroborated by his slip in describing the setting of the dream as a "republic-public bathroom," "republic" being a possible reference to his mother. This dream, then, seems similar to the abortion fantasy discussed in the previous section, in that it allows Eric to invoke the mother as a way of frustrating the other's desire for what he has to offer.

[10] See Eric's description of the drawer: "It was bright. Reflection. A glare from it being so white and clean."

Eric had found a way to become "playful"[11] in therapy, at least in his dream.

Marking Territory

Eric's next session seemed to refer again to the tension indicated in the dream discussed previously: How is he to give me the gift of exposing himself to me, while at the same time remaining intact, protected from the threat of having me penetrate his defenses? Put another way: If he gives me the baby, what will he have left? Upon beginning the session, Eric told me about a television program he had watched about "life-changing moments." As he had watched, he decided to make a note of his own such moment, which he now had taken from his shirt pocket and was reading from. He told me the story of his missed callback after his mother's commentary about his prospects as an actor. He had planned to return in the fall to California, but during that summer, he met Elaine, who as they were falling in love revealed to Eric that she had recently been diagnosed with her heart disorder. As a result, Eric decided not to return to California in order to be with and care for Elaine.

Having finished the story, Eric crumpled the piece of paper upon which he had jotted it down and threw it at me, hitting me squarely in the face.

I had a number of options as to how to react here. Certainly, there was at that moment no shortage of affect in the room, nor indeed inside of me, as I was caught between feeling moved by the pathos of the story and feeling angry at having the paper thrown at me. Would an exploration of his effect upon me be in order? One legitimate intervention here would have been to explore what Eric had wanted me to feel, using my actual feelings as a guide; I could ask him what effect he had wanted to have upon me, and then explore what that meant for him. Another possibility would have been to take his action as a communication of what

[11] See Eric's description of his dogs' interactions: "But so far, it's just *playful*. The big dog does tease him, so they *can* interact."

life is consciously like for him: that he feels profoundly belittled and frustrated at the fact that he is not taken seriously, perhaps. A slightly more risky, but possibly more impactful move might involve me taking my own affect as a reliable barometer for what Eric himself was feeling, but had split off onto the figure of the therapist via projective identification, and making an interpretation to that effect: "You are unable to handle your own anger, and therefore you want me to experience it for you."

Instead, I quietly reopened the paper and handed it back to him. Rather than pursuing the issue of his action at all in that moment, I asked him what else that story brought to mind.

I was not unaware that what had just happened needed to be addressed, nor do I feel I was attempting to avoid discomfort between Eric and me (although the reader would be within her rights to disagree).[12] Rather, it seemed to me that an intervention addressed, at that moment, to that particular action would end in stalemate. I remembered Eric's dream from the week before, and decided that should our relationship "escalate into a serious dogfight" (which did indeed seem to be what had started to happen) too early in the therapy, and moreover in the heat of the moment, the therapy would suffer. As Lacan (1948/2002) puts it, the risk was high that I might initiate a "cold war of interpretative demonstrations" (p. 18). Yet, I did not want to destroy that "inaugural knot of the analytic drama"—the negative transference—either.

My response, then, was an attempt to steer the therapeutic relationship away from the imaginary register and back toward the symbolic, while carrying from the imaginary realm those charged elements that had presented themselves in the transference.[13]

---

[12] My statement here does indeed have the ring of classical denial. However, I ask that the reader take into consideration that I am anticipating an objection that many psychodynamic clinicians would be likely to make. On reflection, from the standpoint of following the letter in therapy, my more egregious error here seems to have been the fact that I never read what was written on that paper.

[13] See Chapter 1.

In "Aggressiveness in Psychoanalysis" (1948/2002), Lacan discusses a policy of classical psychoanalysis that has long been a subject of criticism for psychodynamic, gestalt, and existential therapies: the so-called "blank screen."

> What, then, lies behind the analyst's attitude, sitting there as he does across from him [the analysand]? The concern to provide the dialogue with a participant who is as devoid as possible of individual characteristics … we [analysts] depersonalize ourselves and strive to represent to the other an ideal of impassability. (p. 15)

The question, again, is: what purpose can such an attitude serve, other than to firmly ensconce a power dynamic between analyst and patient, to keep the analyst from recognizing his own countertransference fantasies, and to enable the patient to continue his maladaptive behavior? Lacan anticipates the criticism, of course, and counters:

> We are not simply expressing thereby the apathy we have had to bring about in ourselves to be equal to the task of understanding our subject, nor are we striving to make our interpretative interventions take on the oracular quality they must possess against this backdrop of [the analyst's general state of] inertia. We wish to avoid the trap hidden in the appeal … the patient makes to us. (p. 15)

The trap to which Lacan immediately refers in this passage is the "negative therapeutic reaction" wherein, given the fact that the clinician may have allowed himself to meet the demand of the patient that he present a personality with which the patient can identify, the patient is compelled to reject any help the analyst may have otherwise been able to provide because "[he] can't bear the thought of being freed by anyone but [him]self" (p. 15).

But that "negative therapeutic reaction" itself is grounded in the process of objectification and mirroring, which are situated firmly in the register of the imaginary. Lacan seems to argue in this paper that aggressiveness, the process of objectification, and the development and structure of the ego itself are all inextricably connected, and posits "aggressiveness as a tension correlated with narcissistic structure in the subject's becoming" (p. 23).

While we are perhaps immediately given to reading Lacan's use of the word "tension" in an intrapsychic sense—the "subject's becoming" is most intuitively something we can consider a more or less intrapsychic process, involving a split between one part of consciousness and another—it makes sense to keep in mind also that *aggressiveness* is most obviously an *interpersonal* tension—one that necessitates two parties. After all, there must be a second person[14] toward whom the person in question is manifesting her aggressiveness, and who will indeed react in one way or another in accordance with the aggressive display. In line with this secondary reading of "tension" as interpersonal, we can also (re)locate its "correlat[ion] with narcissistic structure in the subject's becoming" interpersonally.

In "The Mirror Stage" (1949/2002), Lacan posits that the ego is constituted of whatever small, distorted fraction of the subject is reflected and recognized in the mirror image (be that the literal mirror image or the other "reflections" of the child that are given by his environment). As a result, the recognition of the "I" is fundamentally misrecognition or a misapprehension: it takes a decontextualized piece of the subject for the whole. This in turn helps to create the "split subject," more unconscious than conscious, more disowned than averred by experience, constituted of an "other" and an "Other." Hence the development of the subject is dependent, of course, upon a narcissistic process—the splitting off of the ego.

Aggressiveness is a logical extension of this process.

The development of the ego, and its functionality in general, are necessarily bound to the rules of identification and rivalry—indeed, the fundamental questions that structure the ego are: What reflects me, and what is not-me? Where do I recognize

[14] Or personlike object.

myself, and where do I reinforce that recognition by recognizing that which is not-myself?[15]

In aggressiveness, the role of the mirror is taken on by the other person, who becomes an imaginary "other" ("one like me/one who shows me who I am by being not like me"). Or perhaps better put, when another person becomes an imaginary "other," or a mirror, aggressiveness is one of two possible results, its complement being identification. But upon close examination, we find aggressiveness even in identification. Intrapsychically, "it might be said that at every instant [man] constitutes his world by committing suicide," says Lacan (1949, p. 29).

The formation of the ego is, as we know, achieved by negation, but not simply negation of what exists "within" the subject.[16] Not only must the ego say "anything other than the two-dimensional unity I see in this mirror is not me" to keep itself intact. It must also negate *any Otherness of the mirror or mirror image itself.* The mirror must have no existence for itself. Rather it is there to reflect the ego; for all practical purposes it *is* the ego.[17] In other words, to be a mirror, the mirror has to be nothing else, just as to be an ego the subject must be largely negated. The subject, in accordance with the demand of the mirror to identify only with the two-dimensional gestalt of the reflection, does violence to itself; and must, in turn, do the same kind of violence to the mirror. It is, after all, a mirror.

Little wonder, then, that Lacan (1948/2002) describes the ego as having a "paranoiac structure" (p. 21). With so much negated,

---

[15] The very fact that such comparisons can be made betrays the fundamental similarity between the "me" and the "not-me," thus distinguishing this instance from the encounter with the radical Other (as language and the unconscious), with which no easy comparison can be made by the ego.

[16] This discourse of "within" and "outside" the subject/person is obviously a gross oversimplification, not only of Lacan, but of psychological theory in general. That said, however, I will employ this language here for the sake of brevity, rather than making a detailed excursion into the subtle differences between the "intrapsychic/extrapsychic" distinction and the "inside/outside" distinction.

[17] Holding a young child before a mirror, an adult will ask, "Where is little Eric?" and the child will point not at his own body, but at the mirror image.

consigned to the unconscious, there will be plenty that is "out to get" the ego via internally generated or "neurotic" anxiety (which Freud distinguishes from "objective anxiety"). The ego is then caught up in the perpetual (and losing) battle against that which has been disowned. This battle is carried out via its various defenses, among them the mechanism of projection, by which the ego "cast[s] out onto the world the disorder that constitutes its being" (p. 21). The violence done to the mirror constitutes it as an ideal "blank screen" for this mechanism. Hence, we are faced with an ego that is paranoid intrapsychically as well as extrapsychically.

The role of the mirror can be, and often is, played by other people. When this occurs, that is, when there exists an imaginary identification or rivalry, a similar process of splitting off and subsequent paranoia must be part and parcel of that process. "Thus," says Lacan (1948/2002), "the two moments, when the subject negates himself and when he accuses the other, become indistinguishable" (p. 21). This is due to the two processes described previously: the stripping down of the subject and the other to ego and mirror, and the defense of projection, for which the imaginary other makes an excellent foil.

This process culminates in the statement: "What happens to me has nothing to do with what I am. There's nothing about you that is worthwhile" (p. 21). Here we see the negation of a piece of the subject's history, followed by analogous violence taken against the imaginary other/mirror.

Which brings us back to the moment at which Eric threw his paper at me. It is striking how closely this situation seems to conform to Lacan's formulation. Eric took a part of himself, of his story,[18] externalized it (by writing it down), destroyed it (by crumpling the paper), and threw it at me, an action that at once stripped me of my status as anything but a mirror and asked me to

[18] Albeit a conscious part of his story, to which his ego, in reality, has strongly attached itself.

carry the "split off" part of himself (to borrow a piece of Kleinian terminology).

We might also speculate as to the specifics of the equivalency (between himself and me) that Eric was attempting to bring about. Eric had been thrown off his path by the demands of a sick woman whom he cared about, as well as the demands of his mother. Now, perhaps, by throwing this very story at me, he was acting out the fantasy that he could induce the same dilemma in me: by demanding that I take up his story, he might be able to ensure that I do not follow my own agenda as therapist. He therefore does a sort of violence to that part of me that he sees as Other (the Other of demand, perhaps) and attempts to make me a more desirable mirror, by ensuring that I don't subvert his narrative. What is more, with his gesture, which projected upon me (in the form of a projectile) this loved/hated part of his narrative, Eric may have been attempting to create for himself a new ego—one that is no longer burdened by this story.

Certainly, the analytic therapist must invite projection and give a home to the alienated parts of the subject. However, one must not engage oneself in the imaginary, aggressive process being played out by the client, but rather must encourage the patient to cast a symbolic eye upon this process, and to read himself like a text, rather than watch himself like a movie screen—or a mirror.

So I decided to hand him back his piece of paper, allowing him to decide what to do with it, giving him ownership of his own text. When I asked him for associations to the story, he moved from his attempt at aggressive identification with me to an identification with his mother and sisters, noticing that like his mother in the written story, they tend to try "to keep people at home." Then, possibly in a move toward re-membering what was on that paper, he speculated that he may be that way too. Indeed, he had just finished acting in such a manner, by attempting to keep me "at home," that is, to keep me from following my desire as a therapist, as an avatar of the Other. That is, Eric wanted to "keep me at home" by ensuring that I did not stray, in my questions and interventions, beyond the boundaries of the story he threw at me.

At that time, I was a heavy smoker. Although Eric never mentioned it directly, I am confident he had noticed this. I regularly smoked just before meeting with him, and we met in a small office.[19] Later in the session, in a series of associations to his mother, he mentioned her own smoking—not mentioning any impression that I smoked. I asked him what came to mind about this.

"A dirty habit. Grimy. A smell. My eyes watering; burning sensation. Yellow fingernails, nicotine spots on her hands, ashtray, butts, pollution, litter, people who get to take breaks."

There seemed to be an intersection here between Eric's associations to his mother's smoking (which was led into by his transference to me) and the same family of words that he had used the week before, words that had provided a link between his dream of urinating in a locker room and the competitive relationship between his dogs (which in turn seemed to relate to his feelings about our relationship). Last week he had related the words "dirty" and "oily" to his "soiling" the drawer in the dream. This had brought him to think of his large dog urinating on the floor. This new list of signifiers, "dirty," "yellow," "butts," "pollution," "litter," and "people who take breaks," seemed related inasmuch as they, too, might easily apply to urination. Perhaps by my smoking I (like his mother?) marked my territory?

I repeated these associations to Eric, and pointed out his description of "oily, dirty" yellow urine from his last dream, asking him whether he had any thoughts about this. In what seemed like a change of subject, he responded that he had stopped trusting his mother long before her role in his return home. He traced his distrust back to high school, identifying two events. This is the moment where Eric disclosed the story of his mother slaughtering his chicken to celebrate the birth of his niece. This was also

[19] See Lacan's comments, quoted in Chapter 1, from "Function and Field" regarding what he feared would become "the last word in the transference reaction."

the point at which he discussed the occasion, after his becoming a vegetarian, that his mother made the casserole for dinner, lying about its containing chicken. Eric expressed his disgust with the "oily yellow" appearance of chicken as he remembered this.

As we were at about the end of our 50 minutes, I ended the session here, engaging in a variant of the Lacanian technique of scansion (see Fink, 1997; 2007), by means of which the therapist ends the session on a signification that seems particularly charged.

The next week, time having passed since the heat of the aggressive moment when Eric had thrown the piece of paper at me, I began by asking him about it myself. This may be one example of psychotherapeutic adaptation of psychoanalytic technique. Had this been a psychoanalysis, I might have been more inclined to let the patient set the agenda for each session. Normally, this is my approach. With our time being limited, I wanted to take the opportunity that last week's episode had offered while it was still fresh enough in memory to be effective. First, however, I wanted to find a way to steer Eric into a more symbolic attitude toward it.

"So last week, something happened that I'd like to talk about. You took that piece of paper and threw it at me," I said.

Eric smiled. "I thought you might bring that up."

"You thought I might bring that up?"

"Maybe it's a sign that I'm getting comfortable with therapy," he said wryly.

Although tempted to allow his joke to defuse anything meaningful about this event, I pushed through: "You know, I noticed that what you did was to throw one of the most important moments in your life at me. What do you make of that?"

Eric's demeanor quickly changed with this question. "Maybe I was hoping you'd throw it away," he said, with the sudden air of conviction he sometimes adopted, looking at me intently and seriously. We sat in silence for a moment, letting the affective power of that statement sink in.

Throw it away? Perhaps like the animals he had rescued, whom he had referred to as "throwaways" no one wanted? Before I could get his associations to the words, he changed the subject.

"My dog keeps peeing on the fica tree."

The Propriety of Language

"Fica tree?" I echoed his slip hoping that he might notice it and elaborate—he had obviously meant ficus tree—FICA being an abbreviation for the Federal Insurance Contributions Act—the social security tax.

"Yes. Fica tree."

I was struck by the fact that Eric did not hear a mistake in his calling the tree a "fica." This moment serves to illustrate a larger problem in my implementation of Lacan's approach. That is, when does a "deviation" from what the therapist considers to be standard language qualify as the stuff of psychoanalysis, or as unconsciously meaningful?

When do we move from the usefully counterintuitive to the ridiculous?

One reason Lacan (1957/2002) gives for the analyst's attention to language is the thesis that *rhetorical figures can be seen as defense mechanisms* that point to the disguising of unconscious thought. Beyond simple slips of the tongue, the linguistic "gaps" that can be seized upon by the clinician also include "catachresis [the misuse of a signifier], litotes [understatements], antonomasia [substitution of a proper name for a broad class of nouns, or of a title for a proper name], and hypotypsosis [vivid description]" (p. 161).

In the moment I am discussing, Eric's use of the word "fica" seems to qualify at first as an example of catachresis—the misuse of a word. Yet this does not address any conscious or unconscious intentionality behind the appearance of that catachresis, and the question remains: Is Eric's mistake the result of an attempt to keep a thought unconscious, or is it the result of simple ignorance of the correct term?

Leaving aside the answer to that question for the moment, it is important to note that this issue becomes further problematic when thought about in terms of power: what are we to make of the fact that I have become concerned in my thinking with "correct terms" at all? If the clinician is to listen for deviations such as those Lacan mentions above in the speech of the patient, or more generally, Freudian "slips of the tongue" as evidence of obscured psychological processes, there must be some criteria for what qualifies as deviant. These criteria must obviously be upheld by the clinician herself, yet this fact may set her up as a kind of authority on proper speech. How, then, is the clinician to avoid basing therapeutic interventions on a self-conferred authority over what qualifies as proper usage? In other words, how does the therapist remain a therapist and not become a persecutory English teacher?

One answer may be that the clinician listens to the patient to get a sense of what constitutes "proper" linguistic usage, syntax, and grammar for that patient, whose language will be impacted by geography, social class, education type, and ethnicity among other factors. By getting a sense of the patient's baseline linguistic habits—does he refer, for example, to the plant as a "fica" more than once?—one is able to better divine whether the patient is making some kind of slip.

Secondly, once the patient has begun to become aware of his own slips of the tongue and the peculiarities of his language, it is likely that he will begin to catch his own slips, which the therapist can then join with him in punctuating, thus taking some of the onus off of the therapist to judge the patient's language.

Yet it may still be argued that each of these answers to the problem begs the question somewhat of the therapist's own involvement. It may be more helpful to frame the issue by more fully including the subjectivity of the therapist, rather than trying to somehow erase it. In that spirit, I suggest that the "gaps" in language that Lacan mentions, and the various tropes in language that betray the defensive moves of the ego, are not important as *mistakes per se*. Rather, they may be regarded as opportunities;

interruptions in our usual perception, which make latent information "present at hand" (Heidegger, 1927). These interruptions in the clinician's perception of "proper" language alert him to the presence of a much more complex system of linguistic trickery in which consciousness is engaged. They may be the visible tips of much larger icebergs than any analysis can ever fully survey. Hence propriety of speech may not be the issue at all; perhaps "irregularity" or even "texture" of speech is a better term.

At any rate, a rather more simple answer remains, which served me at the moment of the decision currently being discussed. The clinician can look for the response of the patient to a punctuation as an indicator of whether or not to treat his word choice as a slip. That is, if Eric, upon hearing me repeat "fica" realized that he indeed meant to say "ficus," then his catachresis could be treated as psychologically meaningful.

While I have provided some possible answers to the concern over the clinician's authority over the language of the patient, and over propriety of language in general, power remains an issue, and I do not believe that the subject is exhausted here. This question was also on my mind during the treatment, and I had to make the decision of how to take up the question there and then in the therapy room.

Precisely because I did *not* want to play the role of English teacher, and because Eric did not see his word choice as a slip, I decided for the moment not to press the issue. But I have not answered the question of whether this word choice could be taken as meaningful, and because I did not pursue it with Eric further, I can only guess. It is striking, however, that "fica," might have been a contracted form of "Formica," the word from Eric's earlier dream (previously discussed). And once again, the object to which the word refers was getting urinated upon, this time by a dog. Eric continued:

"He's constantly marking his territory. I wonder if it's because he wasn't treated well as a puppy."

Eric's subject change was perhaps hardly a subject change at all. Moving from an overt discussion of his aggressive act the week before, perhaps unable to discuss it directly, he seemed to have begun speaking in a kind of code about it. Making the dog into a metaphor for himself, Eric may have (unconsciously) been telling me that his acts of aggressiveness ("marking his territory," by throwing paper at me, and his aggressive jokes about me, for example) might be explicable by virtue of the fact that he was not treated well as a "puppy." Eric went on to change the subject suddenly again, although by now I was beginning to feel that perhaps his changes of subject were not the avoidance that they might at first appear to be, but rather an attempt, albeit an unconscious one, to more closely approach the salient issues.

Sure enough, Eric began to discuss a date he had this past weekend with a 23-year-old woman. "I fell asleep against her on the couch. Like what my dogs do to me. … Like a child looking for affection from an adult. That bothers me." If clarification were needed as to whom the metaphorical puppy in his last statement was, Eric gave it to me here. He, of course, was the dog, looking for affection from an "adult." Yet the adult in this story was significantly *younger* than Eric, just as I was. He felt, perhaps, that his only means of securing such affection was by an act of aggression: marking his territory. I asked him what bothered him about this scene, and he described his discomfort with being "needy." This led Eric to recall "living in the bathroom as a kid." Clarifying, he told me that, having been the younger child in his family, playing with his sister wasn't easy. Although he tried to involve her in playing with his G. I. Joes, for example, it was an uphill battle. He remembered his sister humoring his attempt to play, but only technically. She handed him the "Cobra" figure, and told Eric that his "fort" was in the bathroom thus sending him there to play alone. Once again, the bathroom is a problematic place, and "peeing" is perhaps implicated. Certainly, we can see another connection to his dream here, where he decides to pee in an inappropriate place against the wishes of the unidentified others who prohibit him from doing so, as if to say defiantly: "If I must play in the bathroom, I'll pee in public!"

THE THERAPEUTIC RELATIONSHIP (IS WITH THE OTHER)

It would seem, then, that *Eric had begun to analyze his own transference*: His need to mark his territory and its relation to his feelings of abandonment by his parents were both markedly present in his associations. Although he may not have been quite aware of this discourse *per se*, all evidence showed that he was indeed working with these issues, and that they were *moving from the imaginary register into the symbolic*. Further, he was doing exactly what he had attempted in his dream: marking his territory in therapy, as well as "rewarding" me for my curiosity by exposing himself, *but not too much*. Eric's first statement the following week was that he "felt *drained* after the last session."

This part of the therapeutic process not only brings up some salient questions regarding a therapeutic approach to "aggressiveness," as Lacan calls it, but about how one might take up the transference more generally. As we have seen, I did not engage Eric directly in an interpretation of what his paper-throwing act meant. I did not ask him to consider how he might have wanted me to feel about it, or even how this action might resemble his interactions with others outside the therapeutic relationship. I did not interpret his dream directly as a comment about his comfort level in psychotherapy. Nor did I make "process comments" regarding his sudden changes of subject as we pursued his associations to his dreams and to his paper throwing. Instead, I tried to disentangle these things from the *imaginary* in order to help him pursue elements within them that were tied to the *symbolic*. In each case, I attempted to keep my interventions ambiguous and invite him to follow the letter in his own discourse.

This stance on my part might be regarded as clinically irresponsible by some. I might be accused of avoiding the "here and now" aspect of the therapy, and consequently the therapeutic relationship itself, which many point to as the healing agent in psychotherapy. But to extrapolate from Lacan's comments (above) in "Aggressiveness in Psychoanalysis," engaging the aggressive act as something happening between a "you" and a "me" will necessarily be a dead-end street, since this kind of imaginary engagement has as its telos a *stopping* of speech (because it reinforces the radical negation of much of the subject, as well as the other) rather than an invitation for fuller speech. Engaging his act (or his dream) *as aggressive* can only mean meeting his aggressiveness with my own: an aggressive interpretation, for example, which strips down all possible meanings of a given act or piece of discourse to one (that one, of course, being the one *I* provide).

I discussed this theoretical aspect in greater detail previously. The more pressing question now might be: Was this stance effective? I would argue that it was at least followed by results that imply its efficaciousness on several fronts.

First, Eric used these moments (the dream, the paper throwing, and the subject changes) as opportunities to associate further and speak more, thus deepening his investment in his own psychotherapeutic process. In subsequent sessions, the marking of territory was fruitfully explored in terms much more concrete and salient to his own history.

Second, Eric explicated something about the nature of his own transference to me as a result of his freedom to follow his associations, whether or not he was fully conscious of this explication.

Finally, very soon after this explication, Eric was able to make a change in his enmeshed relationship with his ex-girlfriend. Two weeks after the last session I've described, Eric decided to stop sleeping in the same bed as Elaine. A week before, he had begun to date a woman who had given him an "ultimatum" to choose between continuing to date her and continuing to sleep in the same bed as Elaine. Eric decided that to change this situation, it would have to be a decision he made "for [him]self." "On Monday, I asked Elaine: 'Why do we still sleep in the same bed?'… We agreed to sleep in separate beds." Arguably, what happened here was that *despite not having consciously thematized it as such*, his ability to state that his "neediness" for physical contact (such as sleeping with Elaine) was perhaps symptomatic of other issues (possibly related to childhood desires or fantasies). What those issues were was not necessarily important yet, compared to the fact that Eric was able to see that *there may have been more* to his discourse than met the eye. In other words, Eric had begun to recognize the Other in his own narrative.

5
Organa Non Grata

> [T]he power of pure loss emerges from the residue of an obliteration.
>
> **—Lacan (1958, p. 691)**

WHAT IS THE PHALLUS?

The notion of the *phallus* is one of Lacan's more difficult theoretical formulations. There is a great deal of discussion and debate around precisely what Lacan meant by "phallus" in his work, and therefore it is not simple to evaluate what it means to charge him with phallocentrism (see, for example, Butler, 1993). If Lacan does not mean the real organ *penis*, when he refers to the phallus—and his writings seem to bear out the contention that he does not, as we will see—then the charge of phallocentrism has much more complex ramifications than we might otherwise think. In this chapter, however, I aim to demonstrate clinical applications of some aspects of Lacan's concept of the phallus to a real-life patient. Perhaps this will help to inform the reader's thinking on the matter of Lacan's phallocentrism in a supplementary way, but in fact I have no agenda in this regard. The question remains open for me.

The following chapter seeks primarily to continue my narrative of following the letter of the patient's language. This time, however, I will discuss the way in which I listened on the staff of the patient's linguistic score that we might label "Phallus."

Following a brief exposition of some basic elements of Lacan's theory of the phallus, which will by no means be exhaustive and which others have already commented upon much more extensively than I will here (see, for example, Butler, 1993; Fink, 1995, 1997, 2004; Goldman, 2004; Lacan, 2006), I will discuss in some detail this one element of Steve's therapy: following the letter as it leads to the phallus, and following the manifestations of the phallus to the letter. I will place a central emphasis upon the process by which the loss of the imaginary phallus is transformed into an articulation of the symbolic phallus. I will explain these terms in the theoretical comments below.

The Imaginary Phallus

To start with a simple definition: We will take the term *imaginary phallus* to mean the *image* of the genitalia, as reflected back to a person in a mirror image, for example. I take this to refer to the genitals of any gender. Lacan's rather bizarre shorthand refers to this entity as: φ (lowercase phi).

The first complication to this notion of the phallus, though, is that we are *alienated* from this imaginary phallus at an early age. The genitalia as instrument of masturbation is tabooed, usually by the parents, as are the genitals as a means of interpersonal pleasure, or of relationship to another person. This taboo translates into the child's experience of its own body, thus "negativizing" (see Fink, 2004, p. 136) the image of the genitals—erasing it, in effect. The imaginary phallus is one of the casualties of the mirror stage, disowned for the sake of the child's conformity to parental expectations. To put it more simply, the phallus disappears from the child's image of its body, for the sake of its parents. This is probably all the more dramatically true in the case of girls, who are frequently literally taught that they have "nothing," or a "hole" where boys have "something," and are systematically and systemically shamed for deriving any pleasure from the vulva and clitoris.[1]

However, this experience of negativization is plausible also in the case of boys, who have been historically and are commonly still threatened in Western culture with castration as a punishment for "self-abuse," and whose genital pleasure is often surrounded by active disapproval or mysterious silence in families, making of it a nonentity either potentially (via threat) or practically (due to internalization of the taboo) (Frankel, 2003). Often, the threat of castration comes not only in the form of a threatened loss of the penis for boys, but in the form of a loss of other faculties or body parts. G. Stanley Hall, for example, recalled being regaled as a boy by stories of "a youth who abused himself and sinned with lewd women and as a result had a disease that ate his nose away until there were only two flat holes in his face for nostrils, and who also became an idiot" (as cited in Frankel, 2002, p. 310).

This pressure brought to bear by the silence and discourse of the parents and culture regarding the child's genitalia results in the *deletion* of the phallus from the imaginary body. As Fink (2004) notes, "the genital region is connoted negatively in the child's image of itself as desired by its parents" (p. 136). That is, the genitals go missing from any sense the child has of himself as decent or desirable; his is a body with a missing piece, as it were. The conspicuous absence in the children's song "Head, Shoulders, Knees, and Toes" is a case in point.

The genital pleasure of boys, like their first ejaculations, is "greeted with anxious silence in contemporary America" (Frankel, 2002, p. 308), and discourse with female children about even the anatomical existence and structure of the genitalia seems often to be prevented by "parents' anxieties about acknowledging the female child as a sexual individual who has pleasure with her genitals" (Lerner, 1988, p. 38). Lerner points out that "not only do

[1] Indeed, women are seldom even told the name of their external genitalia (vulva and clitoris) and are instead taught that they have only a "vagina." For a clinically and socially astute discussion of this phenomenon, see Lerner (1988).

parents fail to tell their daughters that they have a vulva which includes a clitoris, but … the very idea of such communication produces a curious reaction of embarrassment and discomfort in the parent" (p. 35).

The imaginary phallus, then, becomes invisible and unspeakable. As one patient of Lerner's stated: "What I had that felt good didn't have a name. It wasn't supposed to exist" (p. 32). It has disappeared, something like a political dissident in an oppressive regime, and we are alienated from it. Yet we are prohibited also from drawing any attention to the missing organ itself—or more precisely, to the fact that this disappearance has even occurred—via speech. The genitals take on the value of *organa non grata*, so to speak. The genital region is a site of alienation, of loss, but even our ability to speak about that loss is lost. Lacan refers to this disappeared imaginary phallus as: $-\varphi$.

Because the phallus is unnamed and unspeakable, its *absence* from the child's self-image is also unnamed, and because unnamed, *unthinkable*.[2] This sets the stage for the work of therapy which can, among other things, be the symbolization of this loss, rendering the previously unnamed and unthinkable, thinkable.

The Symbolic Phallus

If the child were able to name that absence, Fink (2004) points out, he should be able to transform it into something "positive," if only by virtue of making it speakable. An amorphous—but still tangible—absence might become an articulated *loss*: "language has the power to alleviate the oppressive weight of absence by the very process of naming and signifying it" (p. 139).

This process of signifying the loss of the phallus (what is missing from the image of the self as desired by the Other) results, for Lacan (1960/2002), in the transformation of the negative/missing imaginary phallus into a "symbolic phallus that cannot

[2] This partially accounts, Fink (2004) explains, for Lacan's use of "$\sqrt{-1}$" to designate the phallus: It is the would-be signified of a missing signifier (–1), and therefore an unthinkable entity (represented by the irrational number, "$\sqrt{-1}$").

be negativized" (p. 308). Hence, "the power of pure loss emerges from the residue of an obliteration" (Lacan, 1958/2002, p. 276). That is, the symbolic phallus is the signification of the loss of the imaginary phallus (written as lowercase φ). It is the *signification of the lack in the Other,* inasmuch as the Other is to be found in language itself (which has heretofore lacked the name of this loss for the child) as well as in the parents who demand of the child the erasure of his genitals from his self-image. This symbolic phallus is written by Lacan as Φ (capital phi).

The loss of the (imaginary) phallus as a legitimate part of the desired self-image is also the loss of primordial closeness to the entity that has become the Other. Part of the child has disappeared precisely because it is anathema to the Other (as the parent or m/Other). In articulating the loss, in symbolizing the lost phallus, we are symbolizing the fact that part of *us* is alienated, not desired. It is our instinct, perhaps, to remedy this situation by regaining the desire of the m/Other. We might then try to find out what the Other is lacking, what the Other desires, in order to compensate for our alienation. Hence, Lacan (1958/2002) says, "If the mother's desire is for the phallus, the child wants to be the phallus in order to satisfy her desire" (p. 278).[3] Then again, if she wants something else (in Eric's case in Chapter 4, perhaps, the contents of the movie screen) he may want to become *that*, to the same end, and thereby demonstrate that he is that which she lacks. But in the life of the neurotic (although not necessarily that of the pervert or psychotic) this project always fails. The m/Other's desire is always elsewhere. Therefore the neurotic is compelled to devise ways to redirect the m/Other's desire to him. Later in life, we see the project repeated, and at times when the phallus seems to be successfully wielded, we hear the triumphant declaration: "S/He *wants* me."

How is it that we can reasonably posit this transformation from the naming of a loss to the wielding of a non-negativizable phallus? Certainly the statement, "I was not allowed to have my clitoris" or

[3] My assumption here is that Lacan is talking about the phallus as organ.

"I was not allowed to touch my penis" does not in itself make one desirable! Yet the sheer act of naming this loss brings it into existence in a new way, and by doing so, makes the situation that has been articulated immediately subject to interrogation. Further, it *names the object that has been lost*, thereby re-creating it via the signifier. The possibility of genital pleasure quickly becomes much more present when the taboo has been articulated, and the instrument of that pleasure named. So too with other elements of the subject that have been kept out of the desired self-image to compensate for the lack in the Other! The ability to speak about what I have that the Other lacks grants me the power to claim it and use it.

The person's consciousness, then, moves from the circumscribed discourse of "Head, Shoulders, Knees, and Toes" to one better described by another children's song, "Momma Don't Allow."[4] Here, the taboos are named; the lack in the Other is pointed out (both the lack in "Momma" and the lack in language, which has until the moment the song comes into existence lacked the signifier for the taboo) and the prohibition is quickly broken.

Yet the person's alienation from his body or his loss of oneness with the m/Other is not entirely accounted for by this naming and its consequential mobilization of phallic performance. The signifier, the symbolic phallus, cannot ever quite capture that loss because, of course, by signifying, the signifier changes and even creates the signified. When we name something (such as our loss) we do as much to change it as to name it. Thus, language gives us a name, but not the named entity, which language never had in the first place.

---

4 *Momma don't allow no guitar playing 'round here*
Momma don't allow no guitar playing 'round here
I don't care what Momma don't allow
I'm gonna play my guitar anyhow.
(The verse is repeated with all the instruments one cares to insert.)

For this reason, Lacan (1958/2002) tells us that the symbolic phallus (he is presumably speaking of the symbolic phallus in this essay) is:

> not a fantasy, if we are to view fantasy as an imaginary effect. Nor is it as such an object (part-, internal, good, bad, etc.) inasmuch as "object" tends to gauge the reality involved in a relationship. Still less is it the organ—penis or clitoris—that it symbolizes. And it is no accident that Freud adopted as a reference the simulacrum it represented to the ancients. (p. 275)

The symbolic phallus is a *signifier.* It can only be spoken of, referred to, or used[5] as such. In signification, the signified is lost. But the signified was lost anyway with the introduction of the m/Other's demand that it become absent from the child's desired self-image.[6] The lost imaginary phallus is transformed by signification into a component of a signifier. "It then becomes the bar with which the demon's hand strikes the signified, marking it as the bastard offspring of its signifying concatenation" (Lacan, 1958/2002, p. 277). The signifier overwrites the signified—the symbolic phallus overwrites the imaginary phallus.

But this strange transformation of the signified by the signifier, while it never quite grasps the "unthinkable" in the signified, is the gift of language—the closest thing we have to the redemption of the lost phallus. "The Other's privilege here thus outlines the radical form of the gift of what the Other does not have—namely what is known as its love" (Lacan, 1958/2002, p. 276). Reading "language" for "Other," we can take Lacan to be indicating that language *loves* us—or indeed *makes* love to us by "stuffing"

[5] Inasmuch as we use it to symbolize sexual activity, the phallus, and none of the other erogenous zones, generally serves to denote "real" sex, that is, *coitus*. "One could say that this signifier is chosen as the most salient of what can be grasped in sexual intercourse as real, as well as the most symbolic, in the literal (typographical) sense of the term, since it is equivalent in intercourse to the (logical) copula" (Lacan, 1958/2002, p. 277).

[6] "Demand in itself bears on something other than the satisfaction it calls for. It is a demand for presence or absence. This is what the primordial relationship with the mother manifests" (Lacan, 1958/2002, p. 276).

our bodies with its signification (Lacan, 1957/2002).[7] Language loves us by giving us what it does not have[8] —the elusive (symbolic) phallus. The symbolic phallus acts then as a "copula" not only between sexual partners, but at a much more abstract level between the signifier and the signified body. The symbolic phallus "copulates" with the body (Lacan, 1958/2002, p. 277), impregnating it with meaning.

The difficulty is that many, if not most people never articulate such a loss. It is not until someone enters therapy or reads a book like *The Vagina Monologues* (Ensler, 2001) that the kind of castration we are discussing here comes to any sort of consciousness. The imaginary phallus may see many incarnations in cars, clothing, jewelry, or advanced degrees, for example, but all of these things can be negativized, for the person is trying to resuscitate the phallus in the face of the unthinkable. Many of us therefore become locked in a cycle of repetitions of having and losing, yet never knowing what it is we have or lose.

Steve's was arguably such a case—a case of a loss that was heretofore unarticulated and therefore unthinkable, and which kept him from claiming any of the symbolic phallic power that would have been necessary for him to free himself from the stagnation he had been experiencing in life. In this chapter I will relate the process by which he came to an affectively powerful series of realizations and changes in his life via our exploration of his chain of signification. That is, I will trace the passion by which the negativized imaginary phallus began to transform into the non-negativizable symbolic phallus.

---

[7] Lacan (1975/1998) states in Seminar XX that "love is a sign one is changing discourses" (p. 16). He also suggests that "love makes up for the absence of the sexual relationship" (p. 39), which may be intelligible in terms of our usage here, which casts love as signification and the phallus as a signifier.

[8] Fink (2004) states that "[t]he phallus is the signifier that designates … the relationship or, better, the nonrelationship between the signifier and the signified" (p. 135). Perhaps the phallus designates this nonrelationship by virtue of the fact that it serves as a basic example of it. See Lacan (2002): "The phallus is the privileged signifier of this mark in which the role of Logos is wedded to the advent of desire" (p. 277).

THE CASE OF STEVE AND THE TRANSFORMATION OF THE PHALLUS

Steven Richard Boddle, a gruff, heavy-set, working-class man in his 30s, came to therapy, like Jim and Eric, and like many of us, because he was stuck. But clinically speaking, he suffered various symptoms of depression, anxiety, and dissociation. A talented pianist since his childhood, he had been shamed subtly and not so subtly by his family for his desire to play music for many years, encouraged instead to get a "real job," preferably at one of the nearby manufacturing plants. He had now long since stopped playing in any public way. He was overwhelmed by a sense of anxiety and shame when he considered the prospect, and felt that he had nothing to offer a listener. Occasionally, he played alone, or was overheard by a family member, but that was the extent of his musical career when I met him at the age of 32. Now he worked instead in the local bottling plant.

Steve was also paralyzed by fear and self-doubt when it came to women and sexuality, and had never dated anyone as a result. At the beginning of therapy, he was clearly reticent about and uncomfortable with sexual or romantic desire.

Family Background

Steve's history was extremely difficult to divine. He repeatedly insisted that he remembered "nothing" before late adolescence, and his associations to various experiences, thoughts, fantasies, and emotions seldom brought memories from before that point in time. Rather, he tended instead to enter dissociative, quasi-hypnotic states, wherein he began narrating seemingly random thoughts and images that occurred to him without context or history (I will discuss some of these moments in more detail below). At times, however, Steve was able to remember things about his family and childhood that served us well in our work.

The youngest of five children, Steve grew up surrounded by four sisters. Their parents, Sara and Dick, were both of Eastern

European descent. His father's family had immigrated to the United States, whereupon their last name was changed to Boddle on Ellis Island.

Steve's father, Dick, was an alcoholic. The first memory of his father that Steve discussed with me was of his father passed out drunk in his backyard, in a puddle of his own vomit. Steve, who was 8 years old at the time, wanted to help his father, or at least to investigate the situation more closely, but was told sternly by his mother to leave his father alone—that he'd be fine. Steve watched her as she walked away.

The image of his father unconscious on the ground and his mother standing over him stoically surfaced frequently for Steve. It serves to indicate the way in which Steve saw the power dynamics in his parents' marriage, which clearly placed his mother in the more powerful role. He described his father as "ugly and girlish" and his mother as "strong." Yet he also saw his father as aggressive—at times physically—and remembered a number of physically violent incidents he had perpetrated while Steve was young.

Who Wears the Pants?

Relatively early in his therapy, Steve reported the following dream:

"It was about somebody who died. The organist at our church. She was really mean and tough. Her name was Thelma Cortez, and she ran all the music at the church. Sometimes I'd play at the church, and did my own recital there. *She was mad that I did it and pulled it off.* She called it "The Steve Show." She died the following year. She had cancer. She kept going back to the same doctor even though she was getting worse. I used to take food and stuff over to her. Her husband had died. He was an alcoholic."

After a rocky beginning to their relationship, Steve and Thelma became close friends, and he visited her regularly. It was shortly after one of these visits that her husband, the alcoholic toward whom Steve seemed to harbor some negative feelings, died. As we discussed Thelma, he recalled that her last name had not actually been Cortez; that had, in fact, been her maiden name. He remembered, though, that no one at church, least of all Steve, had wanted to call her by her married name, since her maiden name seemed more appropriate to her "tough, shit-kicker" personality. He went on:

"You know, I remember one day, she told me that I had been nicer to her than her husband ever was. This was after he died. Anyway, in the dream, she was standing up, telling me something. I could feel her presence. It wasn't threatening. I wasn't scared."

"What was she doing?"

"Talking to me."

"Hmm. What did she say?"

"I don't know. I know she was standing up, had dark pants on. Dickie slacks. Looked like she always looked. She wasn't yelling, which was unusual for her."

"Any associations to Dickie slacks?"

"Dickie slacks. Masculine, stern, up and down. Vertical, upright, tough. Shit-kicker."

Steve laughed, and suddenly ran out of things to say. This impasse may have been an indication that we had come upon a signifier that is tied directly via metaphor to an unconscious content. From a classically Freudian perspective, one notices that when Steve said the words "shit-kicker," something in him produced resistance to further associations. Therefore, I punctuated that phrase:

"Shit-kicker?"

"She was a real shit-kicker. She was *ballsy*," he smiled broadly.

The frequency of what seemed like traditionally masculine and phallic language here seemed remarkable. Besides the obvious—*Dickie*—there were: *standing up, pants, up and down, vertical, upright, tough, shit-kicker, ballsy.* Interesting that these words were all attached to a woman! It also caught my ear that *the brand name of the slacks was almost identical to Steve's father's name.* It occurred to me how little I had heard so far about Steve's father, and that in fact it seemed up until now that his mother had "worn the pants in the family," just as Thelma Cortez was wearing the pants (Steve's father's pants?) in his dream. So I gambled on a subject change:

"Can you give me a few words to describe your father?"

"My father. Hard. Harsh, stern, bullheaded, stubborn, smart."

Although there is some overlap between these words and his description of Thelma, his next association was much more striking: Steve spontaneously recalled the childhood memory of his father, passed out drunk on the ground, in a pool of his own vomit.[9] This contrasts with the image of Thelma, who in the dream was *standing up*. In fact, in the memory it was his *mother* who was standing up. In both the dream and the memory, the woman was represented as more vertical, more desirable, and arguably more powerful than the man. I say they are more desirable and powerful because both his mother in the memory and Thelma in the dream are the objects of Steve's gaze; they each hold the focus in their respective scenes, to borrow a term from theater. They function as objects of desire—phallic females, or even phallic mothers. They are mother figures who "stand up," like erect phalluses. They have what the Other (Steve's father, and presumably Steve himself) does not: power, desirability, and "masculinity."

We might take this early memory as being reenacted in the dream, with one major difference: the woman does not walk away. Rather, she stays with Steve, looking at him, talking to him, and thereby showing him that he is important to her. In life, too, Thelma confirmed (or conferred?) Steve's importance to her just before her death and after the *alcoholic husband* was permanently *laid* to rest.

In subsequent sessions, Steve spoke sporadically about his father and his alcoholism within the next few weeks stating, "My father's drinking made me respect him less." But such discussion tended to be rare in the therapy, and Steve often qualified statements like these with phrases like "but he's changed since then." Such

[9] See the description of this event in the "History" section above. This was the first time in therapy that Steve recollected this.

protections of his father's respectability, however, seemed thin and fragile, and the sentiment of contempt shone through fairly clearly from my perspective. For example, Steve told stories of how he had "put Dad in his place" on a number of occasions and "yelled at him" at times, one time even yelling at him for not "standing up" for Steve's mother. His pride in these stories was fairly clear in the sessions. Yet he often defended his father as a kind and gentle man after finishing them, almost as an afterthought.

Thelma Cortez's husband bears two major similarities to Steve's own father in that he was an alcoholic, and in Steve's discourse, a minor player. It was apparent by listening to his tone of voice that Steve held the husband, like his father, in some contempt. This impression was corroborated by the fact that Steve had a habit of using speech to delete both his father and Thelma's husband from their households. For example, he refused to refer to Thelma by her married name. Appropriately enough, her maiden name is roughly translatable to "cut," which suggests that Steve's insistence on using it served to *castrate* her husband. On more than one occasion (which I will discuss in the following text in some detail), Steve referred to his parents' house as "my mother's house," erasing his father from the house just as he erased Thelma's husband from hers.

I include the brief discussion of this dream here because it provides us (as it did the therapy) a point of reference from which to further explore Steve's relationship to power, lack, and desire, especially as it concerns his family of origin. That is, through his (probably repetitious) relationship to Thelma and her husband, we catch a glimpse of the dynamics between Steve and his own parents. Further, this dream affords us the beginning of an insight into the way in which power, lack, and desire relate to gender and gender difference (issues that implicate the imaginary phallus) for Steve.

Like Every Body Else: Gender in Steve's Discourse

Thelma Cortez was not unique in Steve's narrative. She was one of many women who, over the course of therapy, were described as "ballsy" or "tough," and who were portrayed as having more familial power than their husbands. Certainly their power over Steve was greater, given the fact that they always figured as the main characters at their husbands' expense.

Among these was Steve's "ballsy" aunt, who had dominated her submissive and physically diminutive husband, and was known for being a rifle enthusiast and teasing her husband by brandishing the rifle and saying "Mine's bigger!" Female teachers, mentors like Thelma Cortez, and female childhood authority figures generally garnered similar descriptions, and stories of them featured much more two-dimensional descriptions of apparently weak or abusive men, or else they were simply single, without apparent need of men.

One such single woman was Steve's godmother, who entered into Steve's discourse one day as he mentioned the fact that his birthday was coming up. So I asked him if he had any birthday memories.

"My mother made vanilla cake [on one birthday]. I don't like vanilla. My deceased godmother was there. I really liked her. She was really glamorous, and an awesome pianist. She had a white baby grand piano[10] and in the next room a painting of a person holding a gigantic golden sword. I'd just stare at it."

"What was her name?"

"Sara."

In this case, Steve's mother has what Steve *doesn't* want (the vanilla cake), but his godmother has an array of things that excite his desire: musical talent, the baby grand piano, and the painting of the man holding the "gigantic golden sword." In an interesting coincidence, Sara shared Steve's mother's first name.

"Can you tell me more about that painting?"

---

[10] Freud (1916) has remarked that pianos are often phallic symbols, and playing a piano in one's dreams is often indicative of masturbation. For Steve, too, "piano" seems to have been a phallic signifier, and it is fitting with the interpretive context here that his godmother would have this in her possession. The phallic significance of the piano is discussed in greater detail in the following text.

"The room was always really dark. You could just see that in its special place. It took me someplace else, *not where I was*, some special world. Maybe it felt a little dangerous but not in a threatening way. *I never wanted to touch it; I just liked looking at it.*"

"A little dangerous, but not in a threatening way?"

"*Like someone tells you not to do something but you do it anyway.* I always wanted it to be mine. Like a taboo."

"What was taboo?"

"Maybe being like I was, instead of being like everybody else."

This short dialogue brings several possibilities to light. First, we see at this point the "sword" (the phallic object) transferred away from Steve's mother and into his godmother's custody; an especially convenient psychological move for Steve to make, given the facts that the two shared a name (Sara) and a title (mother). Not only did she have this painting, which seems to evoke the phallus, but godmother Sara was also a piano-owning musician—giving her a phallic (desirable, enviable) status in Steve's eyes.

Lacan (1958/2002) states that "the signification of castration … takes on its (clinically manifest) full weight in the formation of symptoms only on the basis of its discovery as the mother's castration" (p. 272). And here, indeed, in the face of his mother's failure to captivate his attention and desire with her vanilla cake, we have Steve's narrative of what amounts to the first appearance of his characteristic symptom: looking longingly, wishing for, but never touching, never doing.

But perhaps most notably (in light of the discussion of Lacan's concept of the phallus, above) we find that Steve's narrative here dramatically echoes Lacan's articulation of the phallus as a lost imaginary entity—the *organa non grata* deleted from the self-image as desired by the parent.

First, we hear Steve tell us that this painting was "someplace else, not where [he] was, someplace special." Taken as a description of the imaginary phallus, this makes a great deal of sense: the genitals are left out of the body image and therefore are "not where [one is]." Steve also stated that he felt a sense of "taboo," of being in a "dangerous but not threatening" situation, "like someone tells you not to do something but you do it anyway." This description might easily apply to sexual situations, especially, at such a young age, masturbation. In a traditional Christian family such as Steve's, masturbation is frowned upon. Steve also makes a noteworthy denial here: "I never wanted to touch it; I just liked looking at it," which of course implies that the desire to "touch it" did indeed enter his mind. Finally, Steve tells us that the taboo he encountered with this painting had something to do with "being like [he] was, instead of being like everybody else." Paying close attention to the letter of this statement, we notice that Steve uses the word "every*body*," and not the just as commonly used "everyone." Was there something different about Steve's *body*, then that set him apart? There was indeed. He was the only male child in his family. Being like he was, then, instead of like everybody else, meant having a penis.

If the gigantic, golden sword is indeed an analog to the male genitals, then we might venture to say that Steve is not simply threatened by a possible phallic loss. Rather (even if only by virtue of the very threat) the phallus has *already been lost*, and is being held in this scene as a kind of hostage in the house of his godmother (a figure who perhaps serves as a foil for his mother). This loss began to become evident in a number of aspects of Steve's speech.

Fear of Heights

"I've always been afraid of heights for some reason," Steve told me about one month prior to his dream about Thelma Cortez. His first association to this was a memory of standing at the top of the Eiffel Tower on a family vacation. In later sessions, he recalled a school field trip to Niagara Falls, where he was "nervous because of how high it was." He referred to his financial struggles as a frightening, "uphill battle." He also frequently discussed his distaste for "getting high" (like his father did) and his general feeling of "hanging in limbo" in his life.

After a number of such mentions of his fear of heights, Steve declared that what made heights frightening was the fact that he didn't *"know what's down there."* Once again, we see some possible evidence for the lost imaginary phallus—Steve did not know what, *if anything*, was "down there."

The Phallus and the Fallen Father

Heights themselves, as Freud (1916) has suggested in his discussions of dreams of flying and of climbing stairs, might connect symbolically to the erection. When we hear Steve mention that "getting high bothers me" we might hear him to be saying not only that getting high on substances bothers him, but that getting an erection bothers him. Of course, the lexicon around "getting high" refers back to Steve's father, the alcoholic, who often "got high," just as his father was the only other "member" of the household who was capable of getting the same kind of erection as Steve. Often, his father quickly surfaced in his associations to "getting high." For example:

"Getting high bothers me."

"Getting high? Does that remind you of anything?"

"Yeah, my father. Yesterday at breakfast, my mother's serving eggs, and he's like, 'yeah, this'll go great with my Manhattan ...'"

Steve flew into a rage at this, and dumped his father's drink into the sink. So his father's attempt to have a *Man*hattan at breakfast (perhaps the "man" syllable shows us that Steve sees this event as his father attempting to assert his own masculinity, his own phallus) and thus "get high" (get drunk/become erect, thus reinforcing his phallic primacy?) is rejected by Steve. Steve's next associations seem to reinforce this line of interpretation. As we continued to discuss his father, Steve commented:

"My father was really ugly and girlish when he was young."

"Oh really? How's that?"

"The way he was holding a drink in this picture."

The picture in question showed his father having returned from a hunting trip. He has leaned his gun against a wall, and is holding a Martini in an English tea-drinking style, complete with uplifted pinkie finger. Here again, as in the example of

Steve's prohibition against his father's Manhattan at breakfast, we see Steve presenting his father as castrated, if not castrating him himself: The word "girlish" leaves little room for argument on this point, and the phallic function of attractiveness/ugliness (that the phallus is the signifier of the Other's desire) we have already discussed.

In the following session, Steve spontaneously referred back to this conversation about his father's picture, saying: "That sword I thought was his in the picture wasn't his."

But Steve had never mentioned a sword. It seems, though, that the last week's conversation, which was among the first in which he had granted his father much place at all, had aroused sufficient anxiety that he needed to go back to it and be sure that he deprived his father of the phallus once again.[11]

Another example of this tendency to castrate his father in his discourse occurred when Steve, while discussing what he might have to do should he lose his job at the bottling plant, said: "if worse comes to worst, I'll have to live with my mother in her house." Just as he had omitted Thelma Cortez's husband from her his image of her by continuing to use her maiden name, Steve omitted his father from his image of his "mother's house" in this statement.

It seems to me extremely important to remind the reader here that Steve's middle name (and his father's first name) was synonymous with "penis." This lends an added dimension to Steve's conflicts around the phallus as we will be exploring them here. If Steve were to identify as having a penis, that would mean identifying with his father very closely not only in terms of anatomy, but also via his name—the Name-of-the-Father, which is closely bound up in Lacan's formulation of castration.[12]

---

[11] It's also interesting to note the fact that the sword had (almost) been transferred from the painting to his father here, further evidence of Steve's struggle around the father's phallus.

[12] The literature on Lacan is rife with explanations of this concept. See Lacan (1957/2002) and Fink (1995, 1997) for a thorough introduction.

Nothing

From his earliest sessions, Steve often spoke in terms of "nothing"-nests, mentioning "nothing" where he felt something ought to be. In the first month of therapy, Steve spoke about his experience of a "void" inside, which he felt would be problematic for me as the therapist. He felt that if there were anything within him, it would be my job to find it and "prove it" to him, but was fairly certain that there was simply "nothing" there.

One day, Steve came in with a bottle of water in hand, and began to casually discuss some details of his week, mentioning in passing that, because the landlord had been unresponsive, his father had come over to help him fix his broken water supply to his shower. "I've been almost like obsessed to get the shower done," he said, but then noted that when his father came to help him, he became "anxious."

"Anxious?" I echoed.

"I was anxious when he came in." Steve explained, and then looked outside. "It's raining. Dude, I kissed some girl Saturday night and I didn't feel anything."

This led into a circuitous discussion of a number of topics over the next 20 minutes of the session (none of which addressed his father's visit or the anxiety Steve experienced when he came in).

Then suddenly, Steve stopped himself mid-sentence, said, "I'm dehydrated!" and took a long drink from his water *bottle*. I took this as a signal that he was now ready to talk about his father, Dick Boddle. Perhaps he was indeed expressing a demand for him, saying that he wanted what the Boddle had to offer.

We can see Steve's readiness to discuss his father evolving through the session if we attend to the way he took up the contents of the bottle/Boddle—water—at the beginning and toward the end of the hour. In the early part of the session, discussed previously, he paired a statement of anxiety about his father's visit with his comment about the weather. That is, the signifiers "anxiety" and "rain" were directly connected. Phenomenologically speaking, we might notice that rain is an uncontrollable, often negatively viewed (as it was by Steve) form of water. This stands in contrast to his later statement that he needed water, that he was *dehydrated*, and his taking a long drink from his bottle, as it does to the fact that his father had come to help him fix the water supply to the shower. Here, we might see him unconsciously articulating that there is something he wants or needs from his father (whatever is contained in the bottle), which I took as an opportunity to ask Steve to speak more about him. Yet I did not want to ignore the anxiety connected to his father, either. Therefore I approached him as follows:

"So, how was your visit with your Dad?"

"It was good."

"You said before that you were anxious. When was that?"

"It started with my Dad sending me after tools."

Steve felt that his father had treated him more like a "gopher" than a coworker during this project of fixing the shower, repeatedly sending him to fetch the tools he needed. He said this made him "feel like *nothing*." Later, his father asked him for a *bottle* of beer, which Steve angrily refused to give him. Recounting the rest of the day, Steve said: "Now I can't remember what I did after he left … I guess *nothing*, 'til I went out to meet my friends. Then I kissed that girl, but I felt *nothing*."

It seems safe to say that Steve felt emasculated by his father's behavior that day in his house. By making Steve into a tool fetcher and bringer-of-beer, his father left Steve with the feeling that he had "nothing." The phallic properties of handheld tools, of course, need little elaboration, but it may be worth mentioning that his father's behavior may have said to Steve that he *should not use his tool in his shower*: Only his father could do that. Feeling, then, that he had "nothing," and that he had no right to use "tools," Steve took the first opportunity to express his phallic manhood by kissing a woman at a bar (bars, we will remember, are strongly associated with Steve's father) but *felt nothing*.

"Nothing" came up in a great many situations. On several occasions when others experienced misfortunes, Steve reported his surprise that he felt "nothing." Similarly, Steve would often distance himself from his experience in therapy by saying "Now I'm making an issue out of nothing."

"Nothing" surfaced again about 4 months into therapy:

"I've been thinking about 10 years ago, a kid I was training at the plant. I yelled at him, and I still feel guilty about it. *But the kid kept having to pee* every 15 minutes. I remember back then feeling a *lack of direction*. Like the piano thing. I felt like a nomad.[13] *Nothing* to focus on."

Here Steve recalled punishing a younger man, not just for frustrating Steve's work duties, but, presumably, for using his penis too much. We also see that Steve compared his general feeling at the time of having "*nothing* to focus on" and experiencing a "*lack* of direction,"[14] to his experience of "*pi*ano" lessons, a project in which he felt a total lack of support from his parents.[15]

If we can reasonably take the linguistic connections I am presenting here as evidence for the as-yet-unconscious loss of the phallus, then it would stand to reason that a young man who had seemingly not been castrated, and who flaunted this by an overuse of his penis, would incite Steve's anger—perhaps in the same way Steve's own penis may have evoked intolerance in his family. Following the letter in this example more closely, the reader will notice that Steve never used the "kid's" name. As with Eric's dream of the "drawer/reward" we have simply to reverse the order of the letters in this word to find that Steve was frustrated with the "di[c]k" who "kept having to pee."[16]

---

[13] The replacement of one letter in "nomad" gives us "no man."

[14] Lack of erection?

[15] Freud (1916) proposes that "playing the piano" is one of a class of readily interpretable symbols for masturbation. Steve complained frequently that he had been discouraged by his parents to excel in his piano lessons. His parents not encouraging him to play the piano, then, could conceivably be taken as discouraging him from touching his penis (i.e., being phallic). His comment about the painting with the golden sword "I never wanted to touch it, I just liked looking at it," might be taken as corroborating this impression.

[16] Another allusion to his father, perhaps.

Castration and Real Men

The discourse around "nothing" serves to illustrate that, while Steve's father may not have wielded much phallic power in the family, and while Steve may have felt (perhaps by way of compensation) that he could castrate him, his father was able to emasculate Steve easily. One striking example of this can be found in the following fragment, which occurred toward the middle of the treatment. Steve had been discussing his irritation with a manager he long ago worked with, who had left Steve to clean up after hundreds of glass bottles had exploded after falling on the plant floor.

"What comes to mind when you think of 'exploded bottles'?"

"Dirty, sticky, sugar, red, black, water, glass, liquid, juice, water, soda, pop."

"Pop?"

"My father had this thing about nudity. He would always make sure he was totally dressed around me when I was little. And actually, he always wanted me to be completely dressed too. He wouldn't even let me go in the pool with him. One time, I saw him come out of the shower, and he didn't know I was home. Of course, he was fucking drunk. He threw his beer bottle at me when he saw me."

My directing Steve to associate to the exploded bottles was of course an attempt to open up associative material around his father, who had been for so long a two-dimensional character in the therapy with few appearances in Steve's anamnesis. Linguistically, there is a connection between the ne'er-do-well manager at the bottling plant and his father: His father was a frequent user of bottles, and a Boddle himself, and was the only other man(ager?) in the family. Steve's associations seemed to bear out my hunch, as he came to the end of his colorful chain of words at "pop," which in turn brought out this traumatic memory that speaks directly to the issues we have been discussing here.

Here we come across a lacuna in the material from the therapy. Did Steve's father ever give a rationale for his perhaps excessive modesty? Perhaps more importantly, what reason did *Steve believe* his father had for it? Somehow, I did not find this out; my inquiries were met by replies of "I don't know," and other tactics that evaded my questions, and I was not successful in getting satisfactory answers. I am left to speculate in the absence of a direct explanation from the patient, which casts doubt upon any formulation I can make.

We might speculate, though, that this prohibition kept Steve from identification with his father as another person with a penis. That is, if Steve was not allowed some view of the body of the only other male in the household, then Steve was alienated from the others in the family as the bearer of anatomy that was not "like *every body* else." This might also imply that Steve was not allowed to display his own body to his father, and therefore could not have his imaginary phallus confirmed by him. It seems that he was neither allowed to look at his father's body, nor to show his own.

That being the case, Steve's father, like the manager, had left Steve to make sense of his "bottle" (the vessel from which liquid is poured and the thing/name that Steve has in common with his father—that is, his penis) on his own, and Steve was alienated and angered by this. This puts some of Steve's other associations to "ketchup bottles"—"dirty," perhaps most notably—in context.

These associations also provided us with another link between Steve's recent anxiety and castration feelings during his father's visit and the more remote past. The reader will recall that Steve's father had come to fix the *shower*, and had once again barred Steve from participating. It is not surprising, then, that Steve said he was "obsessed to get the shower done." Reenacting the earlier scene, but in a way in which he could show his father that he had a phallus (a viable tool) in the shower, might help him regain his own power as well as help him to complete the identification he had been trying to make since early childhood. At a more intuitive level, perhaps being obsessed to get the shower done was simply a wish to *repair* with his father the interpersonal trauma that had happened those many years ago, but when this attempt was thwarted by his father, who denied him the opportunity to feel efficacious by making him into a "gopher," Steve needed to take control of his father's phallic item, the bottle—which was also the "tool" of his father's abuse—and deprive him of it.

My view of Steve's relationship to the phallus lends itself to what Lacan (1994) characterizes as a central question in the hysteric's psychological life: "Am I a man or a woman?" This was, to some extent, Steve's question. Steve was plagued in the second half of the therapy by a preoccupation with whether or not he was a "real man." When it came to pursuing dates, he struggled with the possibilities of rejection or unwanted enmeshment, and then berated himself for not "acting like a man," and wondered aloud "what a real man would do" in the situation.[17]

Symbolizing the Loss

About 8 months into the therapy, Steve reported this dream:

"I was taking you on a tour of my house and where we live and stuff. So I figure it was probably related to what we do here."

"What we do here?"

"A tour of my life. I can't remember if we were at my house or at my mother's house. I don't think there was anybody in it. Just places. I think it was probably the house I grew up in."

"What were you showing me?"

"I don't remember. That's all."

Once again, his parents' house was referred to as his *mother's* house. Even in his dreams, he denied his father the satisfaction of a place in the house! Yet there wasn't anyone in the house (beside him

[17] While my focus here is not diagnostic *per se* (for clear discussions of the Lacanian diagnostic system, see, in addition to Lacan's own work, Fink, Goldman, and Schneiderman), I mention this inasmuch as the arguable presence of the castration complex, and therefore of hysterical psychological structure (which will be discussed at more length in this chapter), guided my treatment decisions to some extent. Further, although it is not our focus per se, it is important to keep in mind that attending to the letter of the patient's speech does not simply paint the clinician into the corner of long, abstract, and obscure case formulations, but can lead to a more general and useful way of speaking about the patient, an aim shared with, for example, the *Diagnostic and Statistical Manual of Mental Disorders (DSM-IV)*.

and me, presumably)—or in his words, there wasn't any*body* in the house. Once again, the letter of Steve's language seems important, and for the same reason that his choice of "everybody" instead of "everyone" in an earlier session was important. In this dream, Steve seems to be showing me the loss of the imaginary phallus. The place where he "grew up"[18] was empty; it didn't have any *body* in it.

The Black X

In the previous session, Steve had discussed his fear that a relatively minor mistake he had made at work would result in a "black X" on his "permanent record," and associated this idea with "a flaw, something hanging over you, pressing on your head like an evil thing you did in the past." When Steve ended discussion of the dream by saying, "I don't remember. That's all," I asked him: "How did you feel after the last session?"

"I started to feel upset and everything. … Today at work I was upset because somebody I like quit all of a sudden. … don't know why I'm so quiet all of a sudden."

"What's the quietness like?"

"It's quiet, but awkward."

"Awkward?"

"I feel nervous. All that keeps going through my mind is, 'Why do I hate myself so much? Why am I so crabby in the morning?' I went out on Friday night with a couple friends at a place near my house. It was really expensive. The food was crappy. The waiter didn't comp us."

What was Steve telling me with these characteristically elusive comments? First of all, there were the references to taking me on a tour of his childhood home/mother's house, which didn't have any*body* in it. Following this is his feeling of quiet, awkward nervousness, then his associations to self-hatred and guilt over feeling that the waiter had not given him enough, had not compensated for his lack. One reading we can give to these comments is that

[18] A euphemism for erection, as well as a reference to childhood?

Steve was (in a not-altogether-conscious way) signifying his loss to me in a more specific way than he had been able to before. The "black X" from the previous session that would "hang over [his] head" might be taken as a metaphor for the deletion of the imaginary phallus. The phallus is gone from his mirror image, and is replaced with a generic signifier of some *flaw* (just as Steve's piano playing had been deleted from his life, and was replaced now by not being good enough at the job he disliked). His comment that his coworker had quit also is lent new significance when seen in this context: "Some*body* I like quit."

His discourse was not only becoming more vivid and specific, but had also begun to take on more *affective power* than previous references to the same issue. Before, he spoke of his "nothing," and appropriately enough, *felt* nothing about it. But here he told me rather more pointedly (although still via the unconscious code of the dream) about the lack in his and his father's existence: the body. With this came the affect that is obviously appropriate to a discourse about the deletion of one's phallus from one's mirror image: nervousness, guilt, and awkwardness.

The next moment illustrates this unspoken castration moving yet another step closer to becoming consciously spoken: "All that keeps going through my mind right now is 'Why do I hate myself so much?'" This question seems to need little interpretation. Steve is asking "why did I do such violence to myself by deleting my own talent for piano/sense of my own agency/aspects of my body?"

The session continued, and Steve quickly found himself becoming quiet again.

"I feel so not in reality. Like I'm going *someplace else* but I don't know where that someplace is, you know, Doc?"

"Who quit?"

"My friend Liza. She's the big ballsy one."

Compare Steve's description of his dissociative state here to his description of his godmother's painting: "It took me *someplace else*, not where I was, some special world." In the here-and-now of the session, Steve was going someplace else—which was exactly where he ought to have been! He was regaining proximity to the lost phallus or, more accurately, regaining proximity to the loss of the phallus, to the ability to articulate it. This was evidenced by the fact that his description of his mental state matched verbatim his description of the effect the painting of the man with the gigantic golden sword had upon him. "Someplace else" designates, in this formulation, the impossible/unthinkable space to which the imaginary phallus has been relegated. Hearing this, my hunch was that the person who had quit her job must have also gone "someplace else," and I wondered whether she might be carrying the phallus at the moment, hence my question: "Who quit?" Steve's reply called his friend "the big ballsy one," which given the role of ballsy women in Steve's discourse, we can indeed take as a phallic characterization. So the bearer of the phallus has gone "someplace else," and Steve is drawn to go there with her. Yet he feels guilty and awkward about the prospect of doing so. The question for me was whether he would decide to pursue the matter or defend against articulating anything further.

The answer was forthcoming presently. After explaining what the conflict between his friend and their boss had been, Steve made what might appear to be another bizarre change of subject.

"I was in the bathroom at the Philly's Bar the other day. Somebody came in and I thought 'Shit! What if that was Dr. Miller?' But it wasn't you, no shit. But why does that matter, and why the hell did I think that? Then I realized my eyes were closed, and that you would have seen that too, and I opened them."

Just as Steve's narrative of his dream at the beginning of the session had alluded to showing me his *lack* ("I was taking you on a tour of my house. … I don't think there was any*body* in it"), his fantasy in the bathroom was of a scene in which he could show me his phallus. Not only would I have witnessed the fact that he has a penis, but I would have also seen whether he was closing his eyes while it was exposed. I would be able to see for him, tell him *what was down there* once and for all[19] and even be able to tell him

[19] See the previous discussion of Steve's fear of heights.

whether he had simply not been seeing it all along. From the point of view I am taking here (regarding the transformation of the castration complex via symbolization of the lost imaginary phallus) the above session seems to have constituted a pivotal moment in Steve's therapy. While Steve did not consciously state in this session that he was alienated from his genitalia, we can see that he moved closer to a clear articulation of this loss.

In the subsequent sessions he began to explore more deeply questions about his relationship to manhood and gender generally. For example, he began to wonder aloud whether "being a man even made a difference" in his family in a number of ways, and how his family's attitude about his gender might have later influenced his feeling that he had nothing worth showing to people.

Calling 911

Several weeks passed, and the therapy attended to issues other than the one in focus here. Then suddenly the loss of the phallus returned in the following dream.

"I was dreaming last night about being inside the World Trade Center Tower and seeing the plane hit the other tower. I knew it was a dream, but I wanted to get out."

"What else do you remember?"

"I was trying to decide whether I should take the elevator or the steps. I was worried that the elevator might lose power. I could hear the sound of people hitting the ground."

Even from a popular-culture version of a Freudian perspective, the phallic imagery here is hard to miss. What interested me about this dream beyond the phallic towers, however, was that Steve *saw* the other tower fall, and thus felt that he needed to get out of the tower he was in. The reader will recall that one of Steve's most vivid memories of his father was seeing him passed out on the ground. Did he see his father *fall* as well? He may or may not have, but certainly the fact that he did fall is implied by the state of being on the ground. Further, the World Trade Center Towers were located in *Man*hattan, which also signifies a favorite drink of Steve's father, and one that he had recently tried to drink at breakfast. We can speculate that Steve might have perceived or imagined that his father had been "high on Manhattans" the night he passed out on the ground.

And what about the plane that hit the other tower? One anagram of "plane" is "penal." Was the fall of this other tower a symbol of the penalty that might await phallic gratification? (Remember that, in our formulation, the phallus is overdetermined. It is Dick's drinking, Steve's own individuality, and both their bodies). That is, if the phallus gets too "high," is there a penalty? The pronunciation of "penal" (which bears a close resemblance to "penile") indicates that such a reference is possible here.

Steve was also faced with the dilemma of whether he wanted to take the elevator or the steps to get out of the tower. His worry that the "power might fail" if he took the elevator can be mapped onto his dubious identification with his father. If he were to take the risk of identifying with his father as a man, he might thereby suffer the fate of other men in the family, especially his father, and "lose power." In life, Steve had turned neither to the physical phallus, nor to his talent as a pianist, nor to an identification with his father, either through drinking or otherwise, for his power. Rather, he turned to his job at the bottling plant, where every day he climbed three flights of *steps* to get to his floor.

One possible rereading/reconstitution/interpretation/misreading of this dream, then, might look as follows:

> I was inside my own body, and saw that there was another body like my own, that had a penis—my father's body. But his body was too high, too erect, and on *Manhattans*, so it incurred a *penalty* and fell. I wanted to get out of my own body/get away from my own phallus so that I would not fall too, but sometimes my wish to gratify my own dreams, to be a man on my own terms still comes to me, I want to stand up for myself, my penis still *elevates*, and I want to *alleviate* this by making my own phallus in all these senses "fall," go limp. Yet I'm worried that if I seek phallic gratification—if I alleviate the elevation— *my power might fail*, just like my father's did. In fact, the thought of this kind of gratification evokes the memory of how my father gratified himself

with alcohol, which brings back the sound of my father *hitting the ground*. I might retain more power if I renounce pleasure and the phallus (and with it my father's kind of power) and turn instead to being powerful in other ways, such as climbing the steps every day at my job.

The Big One

This dream alone (if we let this interpretation stand, as it were) would be a remarkable enough moment in the process of Steve's symbolizing his castration. But this was the first material of the hour, and it seemed to naturally lead to the next "step" in this symbolization process (and here we see another possible meaning of his conflict about taking "steps" in the dream). Were the steps he was taking in therapy too dangerous, or too slow? In fact, the past several weeks had seemed to me a bit stagnant. He had often been quiet, or had filled time with what seemed to me like inconsequential chatting. Because it was becoming apparent that there was something important in Steve's discourse about "showing" me things and his own ability to see them, I felt it was important to ask about the current shape of the therapeutic space. I asked him during a silence about 15 minutes into the session, "So, how's therapy going?"

"Good … Helpful. Sometimes I feel like I'm not going anywhere."

"Hmm. Is that anything like life outside of therapy?"

Steve agreed, making the link between this feeling and his predicaments with friends, at work, and vis-à-vis his family relationships. Then he remembered a funeral at which he had spoken a couple of weeks before, and told me that this phrase was running through his mind regarding that funeral: "I'm the one who is not the husband." The deceased's husband was at the funeral, but did not speak. The most intuitive way to interpret this statement is that Steve noticed that he was not the person with the most intimate relationship with the deceased: that he was simply someone other than the husband. Another (just as grammatically viable) way to interpret it, however, is to hear

Steve as *identifying with the deceased*. Therefore, with the dream and the deleted phallus in mind, I asked him, "Does part of you feel dead?"

He nodded yes: "Sometimes I don't know where that thing, that spark went that used to be part of me. If *part of me is dead*, maybe that's why I continue to live my life the way I'm living it." Steve started closing his eyes, dissociating. "I visited an old man from church last week. He's in the hospital. And he's dying of cancer in his, you know, *penile cancer*! Well, he probably never had sex with his wife anyway, they don't have any kids. Maybe I'm a*void*-ing something."

"Hmm?"

"I want to tell you about this even though it's irrelevant. I found blood in my piss on Sunday or Monday. I went to the doctor on Tuesday and she gave me pills for it. She also had to make sure I didn't have an affection—infection—in my penis."

"Affection?"

"Yeah," Steve smiled slightly, by now quite used to my hearing his slips.

"What comes to mind?"

"Two things. What the word actually means—attention, comfort, worth, love, physical contact …"

"What's the other thing?"

"Affection for my penis."

Steve began to dissociate a bit more, fighting to keep his eyes open and making several apparently random associations. He then pointed at a bowl on the table and told me: "I feel like I'm there, but," and now he pointed at a decorative peacock feather, "I want to be there. Maybe it's like levels. I want to fill the void."

"Void?"

"Empty space. Nothing. Fucking cancel."

Steve's statement that the dead part of him led him to live the way he did is compatible with my comment that his dream showed him abandoning the phallus for his workplace (symbolized by the steps). As if to corroborate that the phallus is indeed the "dead" part of Steve, we see him dissociating, going "someplace else" as he approaches the subject matter.

Like the dream about the towers, the husband's cancer (the thing that made him fall) is associated with his *penis*. Once again, *the phallus seems to immediately be associated with the threat of death*. Also as in the dream, Steve identifies with the trouble the old man is in with respect to his reproductive organs; that is (after wondering aloud whether he is avoiding something, a significant utterance in itself), he associates the blood he has recently found in his urine to the old man's penile cancer. This is a major turning point in Steve's discourse in that for the first time, in a very literal way, *his* penis and its loss are *consciously at issue*.

His next statement brought the situation back into the context of the therapeutic relationship: his comment about the "doctor" (a title which he associated with me, "Dr. Miller") resulted in a slip, namely that the doctor wanted to make sure he didn't have an "affection in [his] penis." Perhaps he had such a fantasy about me. This would partially explain his lack of discourse about his sexual fantasies or activities in therapy. It would also shed new light upon his fantasy, several weeks previous, of having me walk into the bathroom while he was exposed—albeit with his eyes closed so that he would not see his own penis, lest I think he had some affection for it. (This, of course, can also be seen as a wish for a corrective experience to his father's apparent insistence that Steve's body, especially as gendered, was never seen.)

I did not during any of this show any sign of approving or disapproving of any affection Steve may or may not have had for his penis; rather, I simply listened and questioned. I could, for example, have interpreted his fantasy of my walking in on him as a wish, but given the system of unconscious beliefs that he seemed to have developed around the phallus, it was highly likely that he would have taken any interpretation as a communication of my disapproval, and probably would have regressed to an earlier stage in the therapy.

To return to Steve's language, we notice the theme of urine here as well. The old man's cancer and Steve's bleeding prevent them from *void*ing properly. As a segue from the old man's condition to his own, Steve stated, "Maybe I'm avoiding something"; that something turned out to be his own difficulty voiding. Then, after discussing "affection" in or for his penis, Steve produced the phrase, "I want to fill the void."

The signifier "void," then, is (as it was in Jim's case) quite overdetermined here. It refers to avoidance of Steve's own penis (its erasure from his self-image, the closing of his eyes when it was exposed). It refers to the void, or the "nothing" in his own life, which I have posited as his castration. And it refers to "empty space." At the same time, Steve associated "void" with "cancel," one letter away from the old man's cancer. It's perhaps not a coincidence that the old man "probably never had sex" with his wife according to Steve, and therefore may not be able to fill the "void" in his wife, or that created by his own gender and sexual desire. This is quite similar to Steve's fear as expressed in his dream about the World Trade Center. The old man's phallus, then, is also *voided, cancelled even before it had become cancerous.* On the one hand, this is promising to Steve, because it affords him a privileged position in which, at least potentially, he is more virile than the old man. Once again, the father is displaced.

Just after our discussion about the bowl and the peacock feather, I asked Steve what it was like to have been the only son in the family. He replied that he never thought much about the issue. I ended the session, hoping that this question would encourage him to think about it more.

Symbolization of Steve's loss, and therefore the process of regaining some phallic power (both sexually and otherwise) seemed to be moving rapidly now, and the next session testified to this. Steve's first statement was:

"I was saying something last week about getting from here to there," he said, pointing at the bowl and the feather. "But I was thinking if we ever did know how to do that, we'd be dead or something because all our questions would be answered. If we knew it all we wouldn't have any reason to live anymore."

Dead like the old man might soon be from the cancer, which was the penalty for having his protruding (peacock feather-like rather than bowl-like) penis. Dead like his father seemed to be that night on the grass. Dead because symbolized, because spoken and deprived of the "real" that has infused the dissociative space of the missing phallus up until now. Steve was all but plainly articulating his castration anxiety now; in fact, he was articulating his fear that I would castrate him as well—his transference from his parents to me—by bringing him back from his "someplace else" with words. I, after all, had been the one who for the past 10 months had constantly exhorted him to speak, which he interpreted as my wanting answers.[20] We can interpret him, therefore, as saying: "If I speak about my lack, my desire (which is also my loss and my castration), I am afraid that you will take that away from me, which would be death."

Then, Steve did speak about his castration, more clearly than ever:

"I was having a conversation with a friend where I used the word 'control' about my father, how he used to control me. How easily controlled I was, by both of them. But it came to the point where I was like, 'it's time to grow up and be a man,' but I wasn't being a man."

"You weren't being a man?"

"I let them influence me. Motherfucker! But I wonder if I'd kept playing piano, maybe I would have been shot in a bar or something."

Here, we could say Steve had what some therapists might refer to as a "breakthrough." He put his castration into direct relationship with his parents, but more importantly, he did so in no uncertain terms: "I wasn't being a man." Further, he did not paint himself as a passive victim, but took some responsibility for his own "lack of advancement" in life. He stated not that "they influenced" him, but that he "let them influence" him. He also named the risk that he was avoiding taking by not "taking the elevator" so to speak:

[20] At the same time, he had wanted answers from me, so this statement can be taken up as both resistance and progress simultaneously.

that he might have been shot in a bar for following his own desire. It's noteworthy that this overlaps with his father's phallic activity of drinking and the danger that evokes. This is a reiteration of his dream about the World Trade Center as well as the subtext of his fantasy about the old man, and consequently part of the meaning of the memory of his father passed out in the yard: *having the phallus (especially in the way in which it was bound up with his father) was simply too dangerous.*

Having spoken—having symbolized his castration in this way—Steve was now freed up to speak about his anatomical phallus. The previously unspoken fear that *if he should have/use his penis or follow his other desires then he would die* had been spoken; and some of the "real" of this anxiety had been "drained away" with these words, as Lacan would say, and therefore no longer posed such an impediment to further speech about the phallus.

Hence, several minutes later Steve spoke *for the first time* in therapy about sexual feelings. He stated: "Hey, you know Doc, I've been really horny lately and I don't know why." I was amazed to hear this first discussion of sexual feelings after months and months of therapy. He then disclosed a strong attraction he had been feeling for a female pianist he knew in a nearby city, but then worried aloud—quite consciously—that I would judge him as being promiscuous for this (never mind for having an interest in someone who belonged to a class from which Steve's own background implied he had to keep a distance). In fact he said that I would probably look negatively on him "having affection for this pianist," just as he had expressed the same worry in a disguised form the week before when he discussed his physician investigating whether he had "an affection in [his] penis." I treated this statement similarly to the slip from the previous week, and simply encouraged Steve to continue speaking.

Steve's Hard Side

Over the next several weeks, Steve became much more comfortable talking about sexuality; there was suddenly discourse about sexual fantasies, wishes to pursue women, and even talk of masturbation where there had only been a "void" before. His language also took on a more phallic tone as he continued to struggle with the meaning of manhood. For example, the next session brought Steve to discuss the fact that an advance he made to a woman recently was "rejected" by her.

"I guess a real man would be like 'fuck it. Screw them.'"

"Hmm. A real man …"

"What is it? There's no definition!"

"Part of you seems to have a definition."

"Maybe that's my hard side."

Steve seemed to be gaining the ability to speak more about his sexuality as well as assume some of the signifiers of "manhood," which had before seemed so dangerous, so deadly to him. He began taking some psychological ownership of his "hard side" that wanted to "fuck it" and "screw them" without being overly threatened by it. (Also, obviously, becoming a bit more comfortable with aggression!) At the same time, he began to see that this "hard side" could be a "defense mechanism" as well.

He also continued exploring various childhood memories symbolizing his castration,[21] and was able to connect them with his current life situation, which he now began to refer to as "punishing [him]self" rather than "being stuck," or other similar, more passive descriptions.

Pins and Needles

About 1 year into the therapy, Steve dreamed about pins being stuck into a woman he knew named *Man*ion: "Those square boxes you press down on with the pins on people's desks? The pins were like that. I didn't know why they were in her. I was really upset about it. I woke up."

[21] Out of the interest of protecting the identity of the patient, I am unable to present these memories here because they cannot be disguised adequately while still retaining their meaning.

"So, square boxes with pins?"

"Reminds me of some office with like, modern furniture."

I gestured around the office, which fit the description, with a questioning look on my face.

"I had a teacher who didn't want us to touch the safety pins she had on her desk, and she told us how her niece got poked with one and had to go to the hospital. I guess to this day it *made a mark on me*."

Here, perhaps we have a dream indicative of where Steve's work in therapy had taken him: There is a taboo, phallic object—pins, which had been made contraband by his teacher, just as his own genitals, sexual desire, and wishes to play the piano had been made taboo by his parents—and Steve is doing what is dangerous by sticking the pins into a woman. This, for a Freudian, might provide a wish fulfillment! Yet, in true Freudian style, the dream can be seen as quite overdetermined. Yes, there may be the fulfillment of the wish to have sex with a woman, but her name—Manion—suggests that at some level, he is sticking the pins into a man. Perhaps this is a sign of homoerotic desire, but I think that at a more basic level, it signifies an autoerotic one. That is, he is investing his own "manhood" with the phallus, allowing himself to have it despite the risks of "going to the hospital" for both himself and his partner. His associations connect this dream to what is happening in the therapy room, with its minimalist look and modern office furniture, and suggest that the room becomes a place where he can question the taboo set up by his "teacher" who "made a mark on him" (see the previous discussion of the "black X" as a mark of castration) those many years ago, and reclaim the phallus for himself.[22]

[22] Toward the end of the session, Steve associated pins with "needles," "mending," and "holding something up." The first word, of course, contains "men," while the second phrase can be taken to refer to erection, and also bears some similarity to Steve's description of the painting discussed previously, which featured a man hoisting a golden sword.

The End of Therapy

As the above dream may have been alluding to, part of Steve's work in therapy may have been to begin to disentangle the threat of death and the expression of phallic value and desire, such that he would at least be allowed to continue to "advance" in his life.[23] That is, the imagined consequences of phallic pleasure, or any pleasure at all, especially inasmuch as pleasure was connected with moving away from those whom Steve believed needed him, were too great (e.g., death) for him to function as he might have wished. His overwhelming fear of penalty and death for having a phallus "left a mark" on him for his entire adult life: the "black X" that symbolized the absence of the deleted phallus. The final months of therapy, as we have touched upon, saw this disentanglement beginning to happen.

Not long after the dream I've just discussed, another major development occurred. Steve, having saved money from his job at the plant for quite some time, became a piano student again, under the instruction of a successful jazz pianist in a nearby city, who in fact had been introduced to him by the pianist on whom he had developed his crush.

His teacher was impressed with Steve's abilities, and Steve performed very soon after in a recital. His parents did not attend, but his new romantic interest did, and he was happy. Not long after, Steve connected with a local jazz band, which began to receive increasingly frequent bookings. The band was able to fund itself for some studio time, and soon Steve had performed on a self-released CD. Around this time, he finally asked his affection-worthy pianist friend on a date. She said yes.

Steve had, to a great extent, if not completely, symbolized the loss of the phallus; he had spoken in his dreams, in the unconscious registers of his speech, and finally in the memories and fantasies that became conscious for him, about this loss. Hence he

[23] Another way to say this, of course, is that the punishing superego had become too powerful.

moved from the position of a person with some ill-defined "void" or "black X" on his body to the position of being able to articulate the way in which this black X came about. Once the loss was articulated, he gained a great deal more comfort with his own literal genitals, as well as with speaking about them, but beyond the sexual realm he gained comfort taking the risks of castration, death, or failure that are always involved in pursuing our desires, especially those which, through traumata of various intensities and characters, our families and culture consign to impossibility. He now held more firmly a symbolic phallus—*the ability to articulate what he had to offer that the Other may be lacking.*

Of course, my explanation for this change in Steve is only one possibility, and there are others that may be more intuitive, and more demonstrable. And of course, I have not bothered to isolate an independent variable here (then again, I assume that if such an objection was enough to deter you, you never would have read this far). The alternative explanations are numberless, ranging from the possibility that he had secretly begun taking herbal supplements that alleviated his depression to the possibility that he was becoming more interested in sex because he discovered the Internet. I invite the reader to consider my explanation, and the entirety of this book, as representing one more possibility.

The Final Session: Piano Lessons and the Fear of Heights

Steve did not stop speaking in his characteristically enigmatic manner, though at times in the therapy I recall wishing that he might, if only so that he might help me feel more secure in my understanding of his case. On the other hand, perhaps part of the therapy's role was to free Steve to be more enigmatic, to open up the puzzles within him that he had been overlooking for years. Recalling his first sessions, in which he had "nothing" to say about his dreams or memories from childhood, in which there was no room for questions, and comparing them to these later sessions replete with their enigmatic statements, surprising associations, and trance-like states that always invited more questions and more associations, I am inclined to think that this was indeed the case.

And this, perhaps, highlights a key difference between psychoanalytic therapy as I am presenting it here, and other forms of psychotherapy. As a psychoanalytic therapist, I had little interest in "teaching skills" that might allow Steve to seem more normal, more socialized. I was much more interested in helping him free his own subjectivity. But it would appear that, even though adaptation was not what I was focused on as a therapist, it's exactly what occurred—except that it is adaptation on terms that were compatible with a deeply felt—and finally *spoken*—sense of who Steve truly was.

In the final session, as we discussed his leaving therapy and the fact that Steve had come to expect his weekly appointment, he compared his experience (because it consisted of a weekly, 50-minute appointment) to piano lessons. If playing the piano was indeed some symbol for familiarity with the phallus, as Freud has argued and as I mentioned earlier in this chapter, then perhaps Steve was more right than he knew. Steve had always felt that his parents had not supported him enough to "make something" of his musicianship, a statement that we might take to mean that they did not allow him his phallus, symbolic or imaginary. Here in therapy, however, he had begun to symbolize the loss of the imaginary phallus and develop the symbolic one. Almost as if to demonstrate this, Steve then thought of the album he had recently begun recording, and said: "If you hear me on the jazz station, you'll know that I made it!"

While my discussion of Lacan's "Signification of the Phallus" (1958/2002) posits that it is necessary to symbolize the loss that has occurred in the imaginary in order to regain the phallus in the symbolic register, I think Steve's therapy demonstrates that this is not a process that occurs in a neat, temporal order. Rather, throughout Steve's treatment we see that the phallus as genitals is superimposed upon and metamorphoses into the phallus as alcohol, or as piano playing, or as the confidence that is required to ask a woman on a date. Lacan uses the image of the Mobius Strip to describe the way in which the symbolic and the imaginary lead into one another, and the metaphor applies well here, showing how the imaginary phallus is somehow tied into and at one with the symbolic phallus even before the loss, the trauma of taboo, is fully articulated.

As we discussed what Steve would take from therapy, he related this mental image: "I've learned a lot about myself, and letting go of things I can't control. For some reason I'm thinking of a gunslinger guy, a cowboy standing at the top of a street on a hill that goes through an old western town on each side. And I'm standing at the top, looking down."

"Anything come to mind?"

"Some ghost town I was at in California. I don't know if it was burned down but there wasn't much left of it. Out in the middle of nowhere. Some old mining town. Gold rush. After the gold went dry the town was all bankrupt."

"So being here today, is that a bit like standing in a ghost town?"

"Yes, but I know my way out. And I've got the gold, Doc, I've got the gold."

Steve was standing at the top, looking down. For the first time (after a number of similar images, some of which I have described here) he expressed no fear or discomfort connected with the scene. I wondered then, and I wonder again as I write this, whether his fear of heights continued.

The image of the ghost town seems a bit tragic. Yet at the same time, he was ready to leave this ghost town: he knew his way out. Steve was no longer beholden to this "bankrupt" place, the place of absence, of void, the unsymbolized lack in his castration. Rather, its contents had been "mined,"[24] redeemed by Steve. Perhaps he had made his own golden sword from it. And the contents of this ancient town that had kept him there had "run dry" (which we might read, with Lacan, as the crippling power of the unsymbolized Real having been drained away, because the loss was being spoken).

Steve said he was ready to go, and I had no reason to doubt it.

[24] "Made mine," perhaps.

THINGS LEFT UNSAID

Much in this chapter lends itself to critique. For example, a basic element of the theory employed in this case—that we lose our imaginary phalluses as children and that one developmental task, with which therapy can assist, is to gain the symbolic phallus by way of articulating the original loss—is never confirmed by Steve in an unambiguous way. I never heard Steve *say* that he was not allowed to have a penis or genital pleasure; I never heard him weep for the loss of that part of himself.

Rather, I have perhaps provided here a somewhat extreme example of hearing the patient in ways other than those in which he intends to be heard. In the midst of so much interpretive listening, one is right to wonder whether the intentions of the patient have not suffered short shrift, and whether my constant attention to alternative meanings and implications in Steve's speech was not a bit excessive, especially given the fact that Steve never confirmed the theoretical tenets behind my intentional mishearings with any unassailable clarity. I wonder this myself. Instead, I have used one area of Lacanian theory (which remains to be confirmed or disconfirmed) to confirm another. That is, I used a Lacanian-inspired reading of Steve's speech to the letter in order to illustrate, and perhaps prop up, the Lacanian theory of phallic loss and symbolization. Whether this is a kind of academic cheating is open to debate, but it is noteworthy that one aspect of Lacanian theory seems to help justify the applicability of another, without much direct evidence from the patient at all.

In defense of the theory, however, we can see several ways in which Steve's castration was made manifest in this chapter, and evidence was in fact in much greater supply in the therapy, but confidentiality imposes limits upon my ability to disclose it. That aside, there is also the fact that this was a relatively short therapy that operated upon an artificially imposed timeline, and it is possible that given the time, Steve may have come to more clearly articulate that which I hypothesized in this chapter. Of course, this cannot be known.

At the same time, the very weakness that I have just discussed may provide us with an illustration of an extremely elusive (if theoretically wobbly) phenomenon: the engagement in psychotherapy of the Other, the Lacanian unconscious. This chapter has shown the therapist in a rather consistent role as a kind of creative mishearer, a listener to that which the ego did not mean to say, and thereby as an interlocutor to a kind of absent speaker (i.e., the Other). While it of course cannot be proven that I was listening and responding to the true meanings and intentions of Steve's unconscious (because the unconscious is a construct that precludes real proof, since it cannot consciously affirm our hypotheses), it is interesting to note the way in which *Steve's speech seemed to sustain my ability to misread it* across more than a year. We might even see Steve's "Other" replying to my punctuations and inquiries with steadily increasing amounts of relevant information. This is only one way to look at the dialogue above, however, and a highly dubious one at that. (For an alternative, see the reference to shaping in Chapter 2). Yet, in this rather strange way, this chapter helps perhaps to illustrate what the Lacanian unconscious, which "speaks" and can be "read," might look like as it enters actual therapeutic *dialogue*, and the limitations (or new horizons, depending on one's point of view) that this engenders.[25]

It is important to note here, however, that my dialogue in the therapy was *not* one that completely excluded the conscious Steve, the Steve that showed up every week and asked for my help. I have chosen moments in this therapy, as with all of the cases I present in this book, that illustrate what I consider to be uniquely Lacanian about the way I conducted it. Although much of my work with Steve involved responding to what I believed were latent meanings through the methods I have illustrated, much of it was also dedicated to the work of creating an environment in therapy in which Steve could place a reasonable amount of trust, and creating an

[25] The following chapter attempts to show a clearer example of what is indicated as unconscious and germane by the letter of the patient's speech becoming conscious, and thereby being more explicitly confirmed.

extremely strong rapport between us. The therapeutic relationship cannot solely be between the Subject and the Other, in my opinion, since we are even in Lacan's view creatures of the imaginary, ego-to-ego relationship as well. To jettison the psychotherapeutic truth that a basically well-established and beneficent relationship to our patients is absolutely necessary would be ridiculous.

This chapter also aimed to further expound on the possibilities for the use of Lacan's concepts of the imaginary and symbolic phallus in the psychotherapy setting. As far as I am aware, no clinical case studies focusing upon the symbolization of the phallic loss as posited by Lacan have been written thus far, nor has Lacan's "Signification of the Phallus" been brought into direct dialogue with clinical material in the same way it has here. I hope too, to have highlighted a bit of common ground between more mainstream American versions of psychoanalytic thought and Lacanian theory by bringing Harriet Lerner's work into the discussion. By virtue of this connection, this chapter also implies the similarities that Lacanian theory might find with the writings of theorists such as Alice Miller (1997), and even the client-centered approach of someone as fundamental to American clinical psychology as Carl Rogers (1995), both of whom centralize the selectivity of parents' love—the fact that some aspects of the child are preferable to the parents over others—in its impact upon the development of the psychology of the adult. Strange though it may seem, I would venture that Lacan's theory of the phallus may be seen as somewhat harmonious with, and complementary to, the work of theorists such as Rogers and Miller. (But I might keep my fingers crossed.)

6

Che Vuoi? The Letter and the Desire of the Other

> I just have to be what he wants me to be.
>
> —**Caroline**

THE QUESTION OF DESIRE

Always at issue in the Freudian tradition is the problematic relationship we have to our own desire, and to its attendant thoughts and feelings. We find ourselves in the position of having to defend against these things in an attempt to maintain our accepted sense of self, and neurotic symptoms arise as a consequence of the defenses we employ to this end. This is arguably the core of psychoanalytic thinking. As Soler (1996) puts it, "it is a very simple notion: There is a defense against an incompatible idea. In other words, something in what we call the subject is pushed aside" (p. 249). Importantly, Soler follows by asking: "What is that something?" and answering: "sexuality." Soler reminds us that the sexual content Freud heard in his patients' narratives, and which Freud traces back to infantile experiences was not a sexuality that *necessarily* properly belonged to a sexually abusive adult, but that young children, too, are capable of sexual desire, thought, and feeling. Famously, Freud (Freud & Breuer, 1895) moved then from the hypothesis that the sexual content of his patients' speech and symptoms was always to be ascribed to a repressed traumatic event to one that centered upon the idea that *fantasy* which is based on the child's desire can play the part of content that needs to be repressed just as much as can traumatic events. Of course, the repression of such fantasies is generally called for, because the objects toward which they are directed (such as the oft-cited example of the mother's breast or the father's penis) become known by the child as taboo. Indeed, sexual pleasure itself is made known as taboo to the child (see Steve's case in Chapter 5). Hence "when he made the transition from seduction to fantasy, Freud discovered infantile sexuality and emphasized the *loss of sexual satisfaction* as the cause of neurosis" (Soler, 1996, p. 251).

This much is well known. But not all defenses against what is "pushed aside" in the subject are the same. One object of interest in this chapter is the style in which the person carries out the repression of sexuality (and, presumably, other elements of her subjectivity that are not acceptable), the resulting symptoms, and the style with which she negotiates the fallout of both. Freud and Lacan make some distinctions along these lines in their differentiations between obsession and hysteria.

Unfortunately, because Lacan's complete works have not yet been translated into English, those who read only English do not have Seminar VIII at their disposal, which leaves much of Lacan's commentary on hysteria inaccessible. However, his work with hysteria can be encountered in a number of his translated texts via less comprehensive discussions, as well as in the work of commentators such as Soler (1996) and Fink (1997). Between these sources and the work of Freud (1900, 1905a, 1909) the reader is able to assemble some picture of the structure and proclivities of hysteria as it is conceptualized, if not only by Lacan himself, in a Lacanian manner. Because such texts as Fink's and Soler's are extremely clear in their articulation of hysterical structure, and because my main purpose in this chapter is not to enter into a deep discussion of diagnostic characteristics, but rather to use diagnostic structure as a background to the project of following the letter in psychotherapy, I will not exhaustively re-present their arguments here. Rather, I will make a brief recapitulation of their main points.

If the engine of the disavowal of sexuality is the fact that the child finds (via the Oedipus complex) that she has no business having that desire, especially for the object toward which she directs it (called by Lacan object *a*) by virtue of the subject to whom the object is attached, then we encounter the question of what she is to do about that object now that she is no longer allowed to desire it. The obsessive's answer to this dilemma is to realize that if the object he desires (the breast, for example) is *not* attached to the tabooed Other (the mother), then he can continue to want, and even have satisfaction with it. It is no longer the mother's breast, but simply a breast which, freed from its attachment to the Other, can reappear in any number of places or with any number of women, and is therefore allowed to continue to be the object of desire and made a means of satisfaction. He therefore develops a structural tendency to erase (objectify?) the *person* with whom he is sexually involved, finding her attractive only for what (s)he has, rather than who (s)he is. Hence, Lacan tells us that the obsessive is characterized by his ongoing project to erase the Other as such, and yet still retain her in order to benefit by what she has to offer. He allows his own desire to remain at center stage,[1] and rearranges the people around him to legitimate his desire and enable its satisfaction. We are reminded of men[2] who refer to having sex with a woman as "getting some pussy" or make other various statements that reduce women to collections of disconnected parts, which ostensibly exist only for his satisfaction. He is therefore able to

[1] On the other hand, Lacan discusses the way in which the obsessive tends to hide his own subjective desire in his relations with the Other. Hence, while his desire may "remain at center stage," it is in the capacity of a performance put on for the spectator, the Other, with whom the Obsessive identifies (see Lacan, 1953, 1994).

[2] The conventional wisdom is that many, if not the majority of obsessives seem to be men, while the complementary correlation holds true for women and hysteria. See, for example, Fink (1997) and Freud (1895, 1905a, 1909).

perpetuate his position as a desiring subject while repressing what his desire is actually *for* (the Other) (Fink, 1997, pp. 118–122).

The hysteric, on the other hand, places herself in the position of that which is desired *by* the Other. Understanding that the Other has his own desires, his own object *a*'s, the hysteric can ensure her own position as important, as viable, by becoming that which the Other desires. While the obsessive must eclipse or erase the Other in order to maintain his own existence as subject, the hysteric erases her own subject-hood in order to perpetuate her existence via the still-present desire of the Other (Fink, 1997, pp. 118–122). Desire is still there, but it is no longer her own, and therefore no longer such a threat as it otherwise might have been; at least, this seems to be the hope of such a defense, whether or not that is truly the outcome.

But the hysteric's strategy of identifying with what she believes to be the Other's object *a* requires not only that she be eclipsed as desiring subject, but that she must also disappear as object *a*. If she were to satisfy the Other's desire, the Other may, having gotten what he wanted, lose interest in her and thereby compromise her strategy for a continued existence as object *a*. This predicament is summed up nicely in the advice sometimes given to young women by their parents about premarital (hetero-) sexual relationships: "He won't buy the cow if he can get the milk for free." The answer to the problem, of course, is to withhold the "milk," as it were, until greater assurances can be made. This means that both the subject-hood as well as the object-hood of the hysteric must (at least intermittently) disappear from view if she is to continue existing. Lacan (1960/2002) writes that "in the case of the hysteric ... [the Other's] desire [for what she has] is sustained in fantasy only by the lack of satisfaction the hysteric brings [the Other's] desire by slipping away as its object" (p. 698).[3] Therefore, the hysteric is in the extremely tenuous position of having to present

[3] The applications of this theory to thought about the construction of gender are surely numerous and far-reaching.

herself as holding what the Other lacks, and yet never quite giving it to him. Soler (1996) explains:

> In hysteria we see a strategy on the side of the object [of desire]. The name Lacan gave this strategy is evasion or side stepping (*dérobade*). … Such evasion produces a clear result: the creation or maintenance of a lack in the partner. (p. 269)

Similarly, the hysteric attempts not to satisfy or perhaps even discuss her own desire, since it is reconstructed simply as a signifier of the Other's desire. To satisfy her own desire would be to satisfy his, thereby risking losing the existential validation she depends upon him for. Therefore, by not satisfying herself, she is also refusing to satisfy the Other. Soler reminds us that "by keeping her desire unsatisfied, the hysterical subject refuses to be the cause of the Other's jouissance" (p. 269).

All of this makes the situation of psychotherapy particularly challenging. As we saw with Jim (Chapter 2), who seems to fairly well exemplify an obsessive patient, the obsessive tends to lend himself rather easily (at first glance, at least) to the process of psychoanalytic therapy. Of course, that in itself can become problematic as it may turn into just another means of resistance—by embracing the process of therapy, the obsessive can neutralize the Otherness of the therapist and thereby avoid any threat to his own subjectivity—but it makes for a somewhat easier entry into the basics of psychoanalytic therapy: association, dream reporting, and the therapeutic frame, to name a few. The hysteric, on the other hand, is not so easily convinced that the "analyst's desire" is something to be cooperated with, and the theoretical outline above explains to us why this tends to be the case. Just as in her relationships with other Others (other incarnations of power and authority), the hysteric's relationship with the therapist is bound to be oriented by the pursuit of the perpetuation of the Other's (the therapist's) desire. And the therapist's desire is, of course, that the patient speak, preferably about what is normally latent in her discourse. Since the hysteric's discourse is generally oriented by the desire of the Other, her own desire will most likely be absent, or covered over, in her speech. Therefore, the analytic therapist will desire that the patient speak about her own desire. Yet we must keep in mind that our hypothetical hysteric will be looking to find out what the clinician wants, precisely so that she can keep that want unsatisfied.

More than simply posing a narcissistic dilemma for the therapist, this "hysterical" stance toward the desire of the Other constitutes a major question for psychotherapy. This is the case because, as Soler (1996) puts it, the "hysteric is linked, prior to psychoanalysis, to the Other's desire" (p. 274). That is, inasmuch as a hysterical subject attempts to keep the desire of the Other unsatisfied, and that in the case of psychotherapy the desire of the Other is to know the desire of the hysteric, we come up against a major obstacle for therapy.

Lacan suggests that in the treatment of hysterical patients, analysts should turn the question of the analyst's desire back upon the patient by subtly posing the question: "What do you want?" (Fink, 1997, p. 132; Lacan 1960/2002, p. 690; Soler, 1996, p. 265). But obviously, for the reasons discussed above, it cannot possibly be that simple.[4] As soon as the question "what do you want?" is asked, the hysteric has found the desire of the Other (namely, to find out what she wants) and will begin to attempt its perpetuation.

This is the situation I seemed to find myself in with Caroline, and the question I returned to again and again was how I might disrupt what seemed to be a pattern of her seeing only my desire and how to perpetuate it, in order to allow her to examine her own desires, wishes, fears, and hidden thoughts. It seemed to me that the answer for a Lacanian practitioner was, of course, in the unexpected twists and turns of Caroline's own language, with which I attempted to put her in dialogue. This chapter will attempt to recount my attempts at working around this particular type of

[4] Assuming the validity of the presumptions made here about hysterical structure.

resistance using the avenue of language, thus taking up Lacan's (1958/2002) injunction that "desire must be taken literally," or to the letter.

THE CASE OF CAROLINE

Clinical Background

Caroline Young, a 27-year-old administrative assistant at a university, was referred by her primary care physician after she became concerned about physical complaints (racing heart, shakiness, insomnia) that seemed likely to be psychogenic in nature.

It became clear that Caroline was suffering from generalized anxiety as well as panic attacks, which had begun in her freshman year of college. Her anxiety had been somewhat palliated with occasional use of benzodiazepines, although it still frequently resurfaced, and Caroline disliked taking medications. Like many who can be diagnosed with anxiety disorders, she had also experienced mild depressive states since high school. Caroline suffered from "unwanted thoughts," which had the general persecutory themes that she was bad or stupid, and often surfaced when she felt "uncomfortable" around her Uncle Bob, who had lived with the family for many years, since shortly after the death of her father when Caroline was just over a year old. Although it would have seemed likely that her uncle had designs on her mother, if the two of them had a romantic or sexual relationship, they never revealed it to Caroline.

In the early part of therapy, she never spoke about sexuality at all in a direct manner, and (like Steve) would have seemed to have no sexual desire at all, and did not disclose any history of romantic relationships.

Yet sexuality had a rather large role to play in Caroline's relationship with her uncle. Perhaps the most striking example of this was discussed early in our sessions, when Caroline described a common occurrence between the two of them. Caroline often stayed with her family during the weekends and summers off from her job at the university. She had a habit of spending time during the summer in the backyard, as she had as a child, on a large swing her mother had put there years ago. Her uncle would frequently show up to visit her there, at first pretending to be interested in sitting on the nearby garden bench. He would talk with her briefly, and then ask her to share the swing with him, which she always did. Eventually, he would have her sit on his lap as he held her tightly from behind for an extended period of time. At these times, Caroline's response was to say nothing and simply "freeze" until it was over. She generally allowed this to continue for about 10 minutes, at which point she permitted herself to leave the situation. She was hesitant to do so sooner, because she worried that this would hurt her uncle and consequently she would risk losing any attention he was willing to give her. Similar scenes were repeated in other places, like the family couch and easy chairs.

He also made a number of comments to her that took what might seem an inordinate interest in her sexuality. For example, he sometimes compared her to sexually promiscuous and large-breasted women on television, and made comments to the effect that she would be a more successful woman if she had larger breasts and acted more "slutty," offering commentary on the size and shape of Caroline's breasts. As far back as fifth grade, he had been encouraging her to dress more revealingly in order to attract more boys.

Nor did he have any shortage of opinion about Caroline's career, and frequently linked sexuality with her role working with university students, making a number of comments to this effect.

Caroline stated that these situations made her extremely "uncomfortable," but never (in the beginning of treatment) seemed to articulate what must strike the reader as the obvious reason why: their sexual overtones.

Caroline in Session

Caroline's anxiety was often clearly evident in session. She sat up rigidly straight, with her eyes fixated dead ahead (as I sat at a

90-degree angle from her, this also meant that she was not generally looking at me) or looking down, and she frequently fidgeted nervously with her hands, jamming her right index finger into the fist made by her left hand.

Caroline was painfully aware at any given moment of what I might be thinking of her, how I might be judging her, and what I wanted her to say or do in therapy, which contributed to one of the hallmarks of her behavior in therapy: silence. Caroline was more capable of sustained silence than most other patients I have seen. On a great number of occasions, she was silent for the first 10 minutes of the session (something I will discuss below). On occasion, though, her silence lasted 25 minutes, or even most of the session. Often, she only interrupted this silence with words like "um," and "well," and "I guess." These utterances almost never failed to make me expect that a fully formed sentence was on its way, but often they only led to more "ums" and "wells," strings of false starts that could sometimes last nearly the duration of a session. On the other hand, Caroline was capable of immensely productive speech, too, going on with rich streams of associations that I could barely keep up with. Somehow, either mode—astonishingly verbally productive or intensely, frustratingly quiet—was almost always a surprise to me, much like the content of her speech itself.

Colette Soler (1996) puts it succinctly: "The hysteric is someone who is always absent at the right moment, who always fails the partner" (p. 269). In our therapy, I played the role of this partner. This is not to say that Caroline failed *at therapy*, or somehow failed to meet a *standard* that I as the therapist (or as another person) had set for her. Rather, she often simply failed to bear out my expectations for her next move, and I found that the more convinced I was that she was about to say *x*, the less likely it was that she might actually say it.

Caroline, in her relationship to the desire of the Other (as incarnated by her uncle and myself) as well as to her own desire, and in her comportment during psychotherapy sessions, strikes me as exemplary of the hysterical structure elaborated by Lacan, Fink,

Soler, and others. The goal of this chapter is to provide an illustration of how a Lacanian approach to psychotherapy might take up the challenges to psychotherapeutic process that hysteria presents.

Chasing Desire

The aim of psychoanalysis, Lacan tells us (1960/2002), is to get the hysteric to consider the question "What do you want?" This is presumably an attempt to engage her meaningfully with her disappeared subjectivity, and allow her to detach somewhat from her imprisonment in the Other's desire. As in the preceding chapters, I attempt to show here how this might be done by attending to the letter of the patient's speech. At the same time, I will follow two interpretive formulations that I had been considering throughout the therapy in order to show how my attention to them influenced the chains of signification I pursued. I will discuss whether these apparently fanciful initial theories were borne out by the associations and connections that Caroline provided, and discuss whether such theoretical formulations are clinically useful. I am also interested here in the question of the genesis of this hysterical relationship to desire—what are the conditions that favor its development?

Course of the Treatment: Defense-less

During the second session, Caroline, who was already familiar with the basics of psychoanalytic therapy, related the following dream, which bears some discussion because it brought with it some of the signifiers we would be working with throughout the treatment:

"I was kneeling in front of two guys. Then, at home, two wolves came out of the woods and two people came to take my dogs off me because they said I mistreated them. I was taking the dogs outside, and the middle of the fence was gone, so I put them inside. Then I see something, I think it's a deer 'cause the moon was shining in the middle—our backyard was cleared out. My mom had cleared out part of the woods, that's why the dogs could jump—otherwise, they'd be smacking off trees. The wolves came up to the back door, howling and barking."

When I asked Caroline for her associations to "kneeling," she was reminded of "church, discipline, reverence, obedience," but also of "helplessness, because it's such a vulnerable pose" especially because by "leaving [her] head at peoples' hands, there's no means of defending against them." She also noticed that in that position, she would not be able to "use [her] feet." She remembered that for some people "dogs" means "feet." Strikingly, she then remembered that as a child, one of her Uncle Bob's favored punishments was to require her to kneel on the floor for extended periods of time. Thinking about the two men in the dream she was kneeling in front of, she said "that's not the position I'd like to be in front of them, but I do care how I come off."

Obviously, these associations yielded a theme of powerlessness and even punishment in the presence of some authority—it seems reasonable to venture that this authority is masculine, given the association to kneeling in church, which happened for Caroline before a masculine God and a male religious leader. We also have the explicit association to kneeling before her uncle.

Beyond the manifest theme of authority in Caroline's associations, it occurred to me that there was a suggestion of sexuality as well. The position of kneeling with one's "head at peoples' hands" is common in oral sex. We also have the peculiar comment: "that's not the position I'd like to be in front of them [her two male friends], but I do care how I come off." We might take this to mean that, although this supplicating position is unpleasant and compromising for Caroline, she felt that this was the only way to "come off" well—that is, to make a good impression. On the other hand, it is possible, through an act of misrecognition, or *méconnaisance* (see Lacan, 1949/2002, 1966/2006), to hear an elision of the slang terms "come" and "get off," both of which refer to orgasm. That is, if the reader will indulge my (perhaps by this point predictably) wild speculation here, Caroline could be taken to be saying that the only way she can have sexual pleasure is to supplicate to the Other: to become what the Other wants, namely, someone who worships him.

To continue with the dream, though, we have the two wolves coming out of the woods and the dogs whom she was accused of mistreating. (It may be worth emphasizing that there were two wolves, just as there were two men and two dogs.) Caroline had difficulty making associations to the wolves, at which point I gave the suggestion to say "whatever words come to mind with 'wolves.'" She responded with "werewolves, full moon, howling, scary, scariness, mean, violent." Caroline's only association to her dogs was that they were the only real allies she had in her family, her closest companions.

Perhaps key to gaining some access to the functions of the wolves and the dogs in the dream are the common elements that tie them together: the hole in the fence (Caroline began to refer to the missing piece of the fence as a "hole") and the cleared-out woods. "The middle of the fence was gone," which allowed the wolves to enter the yard, and nearly allowed the dogs to leave it. Although Caroline could not say how the hole in the fence had gotten there, she did say that her mother had been the one who had gotten rid of the trees. It seems reasonable that her mother would also have been responsible for the hole in the fence. The dogs were potentially able to jump out beyond the fence, thereby escaping the yard (evidence of their mistreatment?) because of the mother's landscaping. "That's why the dogs could jump—otherwise they'd be smacking off trees." For the sake of clarity, we can rewrite the thought this way: "Mom removed the trees and made a hole in the fence, which almost let the dogs out and let the wolves in."

Caroline's associations to the hole in the fence produced the following chain of signifiers: "digging, losing teeth, a hole where the soul is missing, where there's nothing left inside of you. God is supposed to fill that hole, or other people are. But mostly the teeth, a hole in your gum, being all bloody."

By this point, the reader who is even casually familiar with Freud may begin to note, as I did at the time, the presence of images that Freud (1916) connects with the notion of castration. Missing teeth may be the most prominent of these, but we also might consider the missing trees beyond the back door to have similar implications. Freud's notion that the young girl imagines the mother to be responsible for her castration is also consonant with this conjecture, since in the dream the mother has removed the trees, and has perhaps made the hole in the fence. Yet we cannot but notice the way in which Caroline's language quickly pushes our interpretation beyond any facile reduction of the dream to "penis envy." Rather, she speaks about "a hole where the soul is missing, where there's nothing left inside of you." I suggest that these associations speak to the *pain* of embodying the lack in the Other, of having nothing left inside of her except the hole that God (the ultimate masculine Other) might fill, given the right ways of worshipping him.

This dream, then, shows Caroline's mother as having created the opportunity for Caroline to lose her dogs (who might be representative of what was once "inside her" given the closeness she expresses to them, and also of her mobility and autonomy as she associates "dogs" with "feet") and having let in the threatening, toothed wolves by removing the "trees" outside the "back door." If the hole characterizes Caroline's sexual and hierarchical vulnerability (which her associations suggest it does), then there seems little question that the wolf, coming through the hole with his large teeth, presumably to fill it[5] (like God—her missing father?—is meant to), bears some resemblance to Caroline's "scary, mean," and phallic uncle Bob. Hence the dream seems to implicate Caroline's mother as having allowed her uncle, after the loss of her father (perhaps also alluded to by the dogs who are *nearly* lost), to come through the "hole" in the fence (i.e., into the home), while perhaps as a consequence of the entire situation, there is "nothing left inside" of Caroline.

Why would her uncle need to come through the hole rather than enter, as most civilized people do, through the door? And why would her mother leave Caroline powerless against his

[5] That is, large teeth are the compliment to the hole Caroline describes as being left after the loss of teeth, above.

advances, and allow the escape of the dogs? Again, we can consult the text of the dream: "My mom had cleared out part of the woods—that's why the dogs could jump—otherwise they'd be smacking off trees."

In other words, had Caroline's mother not removed Caroline's "trees" (castrated her/made her a girl), the dogs (her only allies, who could be taken at one level as symbols of her own agency and desire) would be "smacking off" them.

In this formulation of the dream, Caroline's castration (signified by the removal of the trees and the making of a hole) serves to prevent her from masturbating—from "smacking off" the tree, which might be an allusion to "whacking off,"[6] an oft-used slang expression for masturbation in Caroline's home area.[7]

A way to rephrase the dream, then, would be as follows:

"My mother made me a girl, which prevents me from doing what I want with my own body, and from feeling safe outside of the house, including in the backyard with Uncle Bob. If she hadn't made me a girl I'd be able to have my own sexual pleasure, and to use my feet to walk away, or out into the world. But now, I just feel like the boundaries between myself and dangerous predators from outside have been broken, and marked by a 'hole.' I feel vulnerable to their attacks, and I also feel like there is a hole inside of me. I can't use my feet, because they dangle above the ground from the swing, or are out from under me while I am kneeling."

The reader will remember that the dogs never do jump out of the yard—they only have the possibility of leaving. The members of the *Canis* family that *are* in the woods are the *wolves*, who in our current interpretation evoke Caroline's uncle. During the course of the treatment, it became evident that Caroline believed that her uncle had wanted to have sex with her mother, but that her mother did not reciprocate this wish. So another approach

[6] This was not the only time such linguistic allusions to "jacking off" and "whacking off" were present. See the discussion of "slackin' off" that follows.

[7] Such an interpretation would harmonize with our discussion of castration in the case of Steve (see Chapter 5).

we might take to the dream is to hear it as an accusation that Caroline's mother made a hole for her uncle to jump into—that is, left Caroline undefended from her uncle's aggression and desire, sexual and otherwise—so that *he* would not have to "smack off."

I include this dream and its (highly speculative) discussion here for two major reasons. The first is because of the somewhat stereotypically psychoanalytic nature of the interpretation itself, (as well as many of those to follow). The question of whether it is of any use to make such theoretical leaps, especially so early in the therapy of a patient in distress is a viable one, as is the question of whether we should immediately abandon interpretations that look too Freudian as being most likely only a symptom of the imagination of a clinician who is, to all appearances, too saturated in this mode of thinking. Had psychoanalysis become a Procrustean bed for me? The second reason is that the dream encapsulates many of the themes that the therapy took up after this early session: Caroline's fear of her uncle, the mysterious but disabling role of her mother, her competition with her mother, her uncle's sexuality, and her feelings of emptiness. This last item seems to be of paramount importance in the dream and in the work of therapy, and calls for a bit more discussion.

If the interpretation I am proposing is to be taken up, a lack comes to the fore: the lack of Caroline's own desire. All of the "id" in this dream seems to have been localized in the figure of the wolf. Caroline's own animals, the dogs, are tame and nonthreatening. Like Caroline herself in reality, they don't leave the home even though they have the opportunity via the hole in the fence. The violent nature of the wolves, their howling at the full moon, their intrusion through the hole, are all alien to Caroline's own experience in the dream. *All the explicit desire is the Other's desire.* As I mentioned above, this theme characterized much of the material to come in the therapy, but also much about the process of the therapy itself, wherein Caroline often clung tightly to the conscious role of a person without desire, who was simply trying to find out my own desire and then perpetuate it. What were we to do in therapy if there was only a "hole" where the subject of the therapy used to be? How could we work if Caroline-as-her-own-desiring-subject was, as Lacan says of hysterics in general, simply not there?

Of course, I am not suggesting Caroline *truly* was without desire or subjectivity, only that she was invested in a sense of self, an ego, that presented itself as such. Wasn't the wolf in the dream, after all, also *her* wolf, whose drive for satisfaction is perhaps ascribed to her uncle or the outside world? That is, the dream seems, in our formulation above, to very subtly suggest Caroline's wish to go out into the world and roam free to enjoy herself as the wolves do. The task of therapy, as Lacan says, was to find a way to put the question to her: "What do you want?" in such a way that she might engage it, perhaps draining the monstrous wolf of some of its power.

After this dream, the next 2 months of therapy passed, furnishing a fuller picture of the life Caroline led, especially vis-à-vis her family, a picture of which the above dream seemed to have been a kind of sketch. It was during this time that Caroline's competition with her mother for her uncle's attention began to become apparent. For example, she related a story just two sessions after the dream about herself and her mother fighting over the use of the "weed whacker"[8] in the yard. The two women tried to pull the equipment out of each other's hands until her uncle came out of the house to intervene, laughing at them and taking the weed whacker himself to finish the job. She also portrayed her uncle as both overly demanding and intrusive into her personal life, although without ever actually making the accusations. He expected her to dress according to his specifications for attracting potential mates.

He also became fond of comparing Caroline's body to her those of her high school friends ("Hey, Rayna's getting some pretty big

[8] Another possible allusion to "whacking off."

boobs, huh? Maybe you should get a push-up bra, and then you can compete! Seriously, I'll take you shopping!")

The Desire of the Other

Although Caroline did discuss these events, she often became understandably anxious when doing so, sometimes becoming silent for minutes on end after making such disclosures. When I asked her about this, she explained that she felt "guilty" for "saying bad things" about her uncle. ("I mean, he was so good to come and take care of us after my dad died. He's done a lot.") When she related these incidents, she made almost no indication of feeling angry or violated by her uncle's behavior. Rather, she was matter-of-fact in her presentation, not making any comments about him that might be taken as judgmental. Yet the simple reporting of his behavior was enough to provoke an almost paralyzing sense of guilt. Nor did she ever make explicit mention of the sexual nature of this attention. As I listened, I fully expected her to say something like "I'm his niece! He shouldn't be looking at me sexually!" But she made no such statement.

Around the end of the second month of therapy, Caroline witnessed an argument between Bob and her mother. She left the scene and began crying, and her mother eventually saw this, and approached and hugged her. But after her mother hugged her, her uncle joined them, hugging her from behind while her mother hugged her from the front. I asked her whether she had anticipated Bob joining in, and her answer indicated some level of awareness of the sexual nature of the scene: "My mother hugged me first. So I didn't think he'd come and do it too." She went on to say that his "hugging me wasn't a big surprise. Whenever he yells and I cry, he does that." She explained that he had been doing this since the time she began puberty,[9] and generally did it after the two of them would fight, as a way of making up, although this behavior was

[9] Later, Caroline amended this statement, remembering that it had begun long before puberty (see text to follow).

not confined to these circumstances. I asked her about her reaction to this situation, and she said that she felt "suffocated when [her] family gets in [her] space."[10]

Again, while she did eventually say that this ritual made her "uncomfortable," Caroline made no direct mention of being cognizant of the sexual overtones it seemed to carry. This, like her not mentioning the sexual nature of her uncle's attention to her body in the earlier session, surprised me. The intuitive explanation for her omission of the obvious may have been that it was just that—obvious. It may also have been simply embarrassing for her to say aloud what was so plainly implicit in the situation. And both of these may be—are likely to be—true. But it may also be that when we as therapists allow such assumptions to dictate how we approach an issue like this, even though we are motivated by a desire to empathize with the patient's position, we may also be capitulating to a fear to approach the proverbial elephant in the room. Put more personally, *I* was afraid to approach it! But such prefabricated explanations for the patient's silence may constitute a countertransference that could ultimately impede the progress of therapy if let standing too long. On the other hand, a confrontational question such as "why are you avoiding the obvious here?" would have done little good for the therapeutic relationship.

I had stumbled again upon the disconcerting "absence" of the subject described by Lacan. My expectation that she speak about the sexuality implicit in her uncle's behavior was not fulfilled. Now I found myself not only trying to find out why this elision had occurred, but wondering how to proceed without destroying the therapeutic alliance or getting lost in my own attempts to protect her from the painful work ahead. A third dimension of this dilemma was in play, as well. If I were to make my desire for her to talk about the sexual aspect of her relationship with her uncle clear, or even perhaps if I were to make my desire for her to

[10] Notably, she chose the word "family" rather than "uncle" despite the fact that it was only her uncle who would engage in this activity.

explore why she wasn't comfortable doing so clear, I ran the risk of neutralizing my efficacy by showing my cards, as it were. That is, if Caroline was to find out exactly *what* I wanted from her, she was likely to attempt to become "master" of my desire, thus engaging me in a game of cat-and-mouse, wherein she would attempt to perpetuate my desire by never satisfying it (see Fink, 1997 and Lacan, 1960/2002). On all of these registers, the therapy ran the risk of becoming too much about *me*.

Fink (1997), in his commentary on the hysteric's discourse, states that in order to push beyond this predicament the analyst must put in play an "enigmatic desire which is the agent that puts the [analytic] discourse in motion" (p. 133). Perhaps no desire is more enigmatic than the desire, in the midst of being harrowed with tales of her uncle's bizarre sexualized behavior toward his niece, to know more not about the content, but about a particular *word*. Of course, in Lacanian thinking, the attention to the word will get the therapist to just as (if not more) fruitful a place as will engagement with content. Therefore, when Caroline said that it was "suffocating" for her when her family got in her space, I replied: "What comes to mind about suffocating?"

"Suffocated, pillows, rope, strangling someone. Fires can do it, time, always having to do something for someone, working, discussing what I'm going to do about work."

"Pillows?"

"Obviously, putting them over someone's head, but they're also on couches and chairs and sitting or lying on them with my family makes me uncomfortable. I feel confused, like I'm not grasping something, and I don't know what it is."

A number of rather dramatic associations came up in this list, but still the sexual element on which I was looking to find some commentary seemed absent. Yet strikingly, Caroline found herself at the end of this string of associations feeling confused, wondering what she was missing. Hence, my primary goal of directing her attention back toward her own discourse and the mysteries of her own subjectivity and desire may have been achieved here. She was not for the moment overly concerned with what I wanted her to do, but was focused on wondering what she was "not grasping" about herself.

Because the word "fire" had surfaced for Caroline before, I asked about its presence here. This reminded her of a dream she had about "accidentally starting a fire, burning down the woods and someone's house, and getting lost." Some of the text of the dream bears repeating here:

"I have a problem with fire. I like it. It's pretty, something I've been thinking about I guess. After I accidentally started a fire in the backyard—because it *was* an accident—it [the dream] switched and I was running away with my brother to a vet's house with a fenced-in yard. I didn't tell them about the fire, just played in the backyard."

The dream itself, as well as her commentary on it, was long and complex. What I'd like to comment on here, however, is the way in which following Caroline's linguistic associations to the hugging scene on vacation led to this dream, and these associations in turn afforded some insight into the way being hugged by, or held while sitting on furniture by her uncle affected her, inclusive of the sexual dimension of the situation, which she had not addressed in her direct commentary.

The association "fire" proved to be particularly fruitful, as the dream demonstrates. Caroline felt "suffocated" by her uncle's (or "family's") habit of having her sit on his lap, especially on the swing, and suffocation can be brought on by "fires." So we might provisionally see the fire in the dream as referring to something about her uncle's presence in her house, or about the ritualistic sitting on his lap. The fire in the dream, Caroline insisted, was "accidentally" started. In her emphasis upon the accidental nature of the fire, we recognize that she is invested in *not* being seen as having wanted to start it, which indicates the possibility that in fact, the fire was no accident at all, but rather a signifier of something she desired ("I have a problem with fire. I like it"). The fire, at any rate, "burned down woods and someone's house." Here we see the return of the image of the woods (which I interpreted above as a phallic symbol, the absence of which in the first dream pointed to Caroline's vulnerability and genitalia, as well as perhaps to Caroline's uncle). This time it was Caroline, and not her mother, who was removing the trees.

A simple transposition of the above series of dream thoughts might run as follows:

Let "Fire" = "sitting on uncle's lap" (by virtue of their suffocating nature).
Let "The fire was an accident" = "I wanted to start the fire" (by virtue of denial).
Therefore, "The fire was an accident" = "I want to sit on my uncle's lap."

Yet there is the added meaning of the word "fire" here that it destroys the trees or the phallus that Caroline might, according to her fantasy, be missing (see Chapter 4). Therefore, we can also write the dream thoughts this way:

Fire in the backyard destroys the trees.
Fire in the backyard destroys my ability to defend myself and makes my genitals disappear.
Sitting on my uncle's lap in the backyard destroys my ability to defend myself and makes my genitals disappear.

These two re-readings of this part of the dream seem mutually exclusive. How could Caroline (unconsciously, incompletely) want to sit on her uncle's lap while at the same time knowing that this leaves her suffocated, broken, defenseless, and sexless? Yet the two thoughts may not be entirely contradictory after all, if we examine them for their teleology. That is, Caroline may have unconsciously wanted her uncle to approach her *precisely because* the scene brings with it a sense of castration and defenselessness. If Caroline is without defense, agency, or sexuality, she is without her own desire. She then can more easily maintain her role as her uncle's desired *object* instead of *desiring subject*. All the desire in the scene on the swing, after all, belongs to her uncle, the Other.

Knowing what he wants (whether it is sexual or not) allows her to be in control of that desire without entirely giving in to it, and having no sexuality, agency, or desire makes it that much easier to not give in to it.

At the same time, of course, Caroline is perhaps fulfilling another wish in this dream—the wish to destroy her uncle and his abusive behavior by burning down the place where it tends to occur. She also goes into the backyard of a veterinarian, a caretaker of dogs (which we have already interpreted as symbolizing Caroline's own autonomy and subjectivity).

Now another problem arises: How could this very speculative interpretation I've introduced, that being held by her uncle erases her genitals, be compatible with the conjecture that she is aware at some level of the sexual nature of the encounter? It would seem that precisely the opposite would be true, and that Caroline would become *painfully* aware of her genitalia at such a moment, even if this only springs from the disturbing realization of the general involvement of sexuality in this scene. So perhaps I am skipping a step here, and implicit in (and logically prior to) the statement that her uncle's holding her somehow makes her genitals disappear is the fact that it makes them *appear*, and then by means of her revulsion by this appearance, *dis*appear from consciousness.

Of course, these formulations were still rather wild guesses on my part, and I made no mention of them to Caroline. Rather, I continued gathering her associations to the dream, operating under the assumption that her discourse about the dream would provide material relating to her thoughts about her uncle having her on his lap. I asked her, therefore: "How did the fire start?"

She replied: "There was a fence, and on the other side there was a hat or a bunny. I went to get it with the stick and when I moved the stick, the fire started. It was very shocking."

"Any thoughts about 'stick?'"

"Stick: bone, dry, small. I guess you do pull a bunny from a hat. The bunny was pink."

The introduction of the stick, the hat, and the bunny complicates the "fire" symbol further. Again, we see some rather sexual imagery here. The stick attempts to touch the hat or bunny, and when it is moved, it causes a fire that burnt down the trees. The stick seems to be analogous to the penis, while the hat seems fairly recognizable as a vaginal image, from which a pink bunny (or baby) will emerge as a result of having touched the "hat" with the "stick" like magicians do. The fire that destroys the trees might now be seen as sexual excitement, or even orgasm, which leads to detumescence, for which the burning down of a tree is a viable metaphor. The dream, then, seems to be introducing the possibility of heterosexual intercourse, resulting in a baby being produced. If this thought is applied to the scene with her uncle, we can see the urgent need for Caroline to insist on the accidental nature of having started the fire.

Again, this interpretation may seem, and perhaps is, a bit wild. Nor will it escape the reader that it seems to have been picked directly from a stockpile of psychoanalytic chestnuts. Yet an interesting moment in Caroline's discussion of the dream (before she had spoken about the stick and the hat) may argue for its plausibility: "When the fire started, we were between two houses like a movie that I remember from my kid—my childhood." I punctuated her slip by repeating: "Your kid?" Her response was to suddenly go blank for a moment, and then say, "I think you think I'm keeping something from you." The fact that this thought occurred to Caroline at all, of course, indicated that perhaps she felt as though she *was* "keeping something from" me, although exactly what that might have been, I cannot say. I might venture the guess, however, that it was precisely the fantasy I am contending that this dream concealed—the fantasy of having her uncle's child—that she felt she was keeping from both of us. The slip led Caroline to mention that she felt "abnormal" for not "following everyone else's plans"—that is, not being married and having children like other women she knew, and *like her uncle said he wanted her to do.*

It may be important to take a moment to clarify the direction of some of my statements here, because of the "incendiary" nature, even (or especially) 110 years after the publication of *The Interpretation of Dreams*, of making such Oedipal interpretations. While my presentation of this dream points to the possibility of a fantasy or even a wish that Caroline may have entertained for having her uncle's child, I do not believe the dream's signification stops there. Here it will be helpful to recall the discussion above of Lacan's formulation of the hysterical relationship to the Other's desire. The hysteric, we remember, constitutes herself as *object*, as a manifestation of what the Other lacks, *in order to ensure her very existence—to save her own life, sometimes literally.* Many levels of her own desire, therefore, are constructed upon, or out of, the desire of this Other—her interpretation of his desire becomes her desire. This is not to say that the hysteric has no desire or subjectivity of her own; on the contrary, this is what psychotherapy hopes to shed light upon and liberate. However, in the clinical encounter, as the "many-staved score" of discourse is explored (see Lacan, 1953 and Chapter 1 of this book), the therapist does not necessarily encounter discrete packages of desire that are clearly labeled "subject's true desire" and "subject's fantasy of the Other's desire." Nor can we assume that whatever desires are conscious are the objectified desire of the Other that the hysteric attempts to embody, while whatever desires are unconscious are somehow more genuine. Rather, we find many shades of gray, which do not easily sort themselves out, but rather fuel the long and unpredictable process of finding ways to articulate one's subjective desire. In the meantime, however, it would be clinically irresponsible not to attend, at least in the process of case formulation, to possible fantasies and desires, even those that may strike the clinician (or the patient, for that matter) as cliché, disturbing, or grotesque.

In the case of this dream, my assessment is that we find not only the fantasy of Caroline bearing her uncle's child, but the fantasy implicit within it of *being* her uncle's child as well—that is, having someone to replace her father. Whether or not he was as emotionally abusive as she painted him, she described him as placing value on her mainly as a sexual object with the potential to produce children. It is therefore absolutely consistent with a child's disposition to desire the love of a parent (and this is perhaps amplified for a child who has *lost* a parent, and now has a second chance with a stepparent) that she would attempt to construct fantasies in which she entertained not only the desire for a daughter who would successfully reproduce, but also the desire to be physically close to her.

The sexual aspect of her uncle's behavior (and her complicity with it), which was utterly absent from her direct discussion of the episode of her uncle's argument with her mother, then surfaced via her discussion of the dream. I glean this interpretation from the context of the dream itself (taken along with the previous dream), and the moment in the session at which Caroline introduced it, in addition to the content of the dream and its attendant associations discussed previously.

I did not make any such interpretations to Caroline during the session, but rather used my impressions to help build the clinical picture of how Caroline handled the questions of her own desire, her sexuality, and her uncle's desire and sexuality, all of which had been conspicuously absent from her speech in therapy. This was clinically useful in that it pointed the way, if not to any grand truths about exactly what Caroline deeply wanted, to an area in which desire was held hostage by an Other. I now could wager that Caroline kept herself away from her own desire in order to satisfy her uncle (recall her dream about sending the dogs back in the house to satisfy the men/wolves who had come to take them), and that this issue seemed tightly interwoven with her sexuality and gender. With this hypothesis, I could continue to follow Caroline's speech with an ear to what it might also be saying about this nexus of issues, attuning my "misunderstandings" of her language to the areas in question (while keeping open the possibility of hearing latent meanings on other registers as well).

Transference and Countertransference

There are a number of stances within the psychodynamic tradition regarding the therapist's countertransference, some of which I have commented on already (see Chapter 5). It has become somewhat fashionable (see, for example, Renik, 1999; Davies, 2004) to advocate a rather free flow of disclosure to the patient of how the therapist is reacting at any given moment: what fantasies are brought to mind by the patient, what feelings are elicited by the patient—in other words, for the therapist to do her own free associating during the session. This approach seems to be based upon the assumption that there will be something instructive for the patient in the therapist's associations or feelings, something universal, perhaps, that the patient elicits in many people. Some lines of thinking (see Maroda, 1999, 2001) encourage the therapist to draw heavily from her countertransference to inform her interventions, which are geared toward the achievement of Alexander's (1980) "corrective emotional experience."

I have heard the criticism made of Lacanian psychoanalysis that it encourages a lack of attention to the analyst's countertransference, thereby creating a dangerous blind spot in the clinical relationship. This may be true in the practice of some Lacanian analysts or therapists, but I am not sure that it is endemic in the theory. Certainly, Lacan does not encourage acting based upon one's belief that one's countertransference will itself be particularly helpful to the patient—quite the contrary! However, I see no reason to take from his writings that the clinician should not be keenly aware of his own reactions, wishes, fantasies, and other associations while in the presence of the patient. My own sense is that these can be quite instructive, if not about the patient, about what she evokes in me, and therefore can allow me at least to avoid making interventions that are based only upon my countertransference, rather than the patient's speech. Lacan (1951/2006) cautions us that countertransference, far from constituting some magical access into the world of the patient, can be "defined as the sum total of the analyst's biases, passions, and difficulties, or even of his inadequate information, at any given moment" (p. 183).

Nor do I think that any impulse to make an intervention that originates in countertransference (for don't they all, at some level?) should be dismissed out of hand. Rather, it should be interrogated from a point of view that recognizes the clinician's countertransferential investment in the thought, and sorts out the possible pros and cons of the intervention from there. If this kind of discipline is observed, it can help maintain the respect for our patient's subjectivity and Otherness that I see as the keystone of Lacanian psychoanalysis, keeping our countertransference from leading us into an imaginary identification with the client and the attendant loss of professional boundaries that it entails. Further, threshing out the clinically helpful from the imaginary in the content of our countertransference, finding whether there is anything in our impulses that might be responsibly applied, might have the effect of choosing interventions that can help perpetuate the engaged speech of the patient.

I would like to briefly discuss what I see as this kind of moment in Caroline's therapy, in order to demonstrate that attention to one's countertransference, and even acting based upon what we can learn from it after some interrogation, can be clinically useful. This example interests me particularly because it deals with my countertransference regarding Caroline's transference of feelings and thoughts about her uncle onto me. Hence we have a situation in which the temptations of the imaginary were running rampant.

Several months after the sessions above, Caroline and I were discussing her experience of a previous session, in which I made a tentative interpretation regarding the possible sexual application of her comments about feeling "caught" (see the section "Getting Caught: The Symptomatic Act," later in this chapter). Her first statement was that she had been "exhausted," which indicated to me that something important must have happened in the session.

She then said she was usually "uncomfortable"[11] with the topic of sexuality in general.

She explained: "At home it's just not brought up in a way that I would think of as okay or normal, so I just prefer to avoid it altogether, I suppose."

"Not okay or normal?"

"Yeah, like the boundary between what I'm comfortable and uncomfortable with is crossed a lot at home."

Part of my countertransference toward Caroline was to worry that by asking difficult questions or bringing up difficult material—especially by broaching sexual subjects—I might re-victimize her, repeating a pattern based on what her uncle had been doing. To be likened to Caroline's uncle was an extremely distasteful prospect for me. It was an anxiety-provoking thought that I, who had situated myself in the position of a helping party, might begin to resemble a person who had apparently been quite unhelpful to this woman since her childhood. I wanted to be the good guy, simply put. Given the degree to which sexuality seemed to be an issue for Caroline, this particular countertransference made my job rather difficult. Now, hearing talk of boundaries being crossed at home as Caroline was describing her experience of the previous session, I became anxious that I had gone too far, that I had crossed the boundary in question. Part of the concern was my own anxiety, my own resistance, perhaps. Yet I came to the conclusion at that moment that there was also something legitimate to the therapy in my sense of worry. If Caroline had felt that I had indeed "crossed the boundary," then several things might result, all of which I felt it was important for me to get more information about.

First, there was the question of how intense the transference from Caroline's uncle to me had become. Of course, the development of the transference is regarded by Lacan (1951/2006) as a positive

[11] "Uncomfortable" was a word she sometimes used to describe how she felt around her uncle. I therefore pursued this topic in order to get a better sense of the degree to which I was becoming the object of her transference and whether this was likely to interfere with, or conversely, enhance the course of therapy.

thing, indispensable to the process of psychoanalysis. However, it can also become the case that the transference outgrows what the therapy can sustain and become a wellspring of resistance that can derail the therapy (see, for example, Freud, 1905a). I therefore felt that it was in the interest of the therapy to see just how much like her uncle Bob I had become to Caroline at such an early point in our sessions. It was of paramount importance, especially at that time, that Caroline continue to feel that it was safe to speak.

Additionally, if I had crossed a boundary, it was important to give Caroline an opportunity to say so, to react to a familiar situation (feeling like an older man had crossed a sexual boundary with her) in a new way (with speech instead of silence). Here we might see an intersection of Lacanian practice with the notion of the "corrective emotional experience," with the difference that the opportunity to react in a new way to an old situation is placed with the patient more than the therapist.[12]

If I had not crossed this boundary, then it might be helpful to know what was different in therapy from the "uncomfortable," boundary-crossing experiences with her uncle. If Caroline was able to talk about this, she might then have been able to more fully articulate exactly what she was uncomfortable *with*, as well as how she *desired* things to be different.[13] For these reasons, and with confidence that I was not simply asking Caroline to manage my own anxiety, I asked the question:

"Was the boundary crossed here?"

"No. Even though I was uncomfortable, you weren't crossing it. Your reaction to my reaction is different."

Admittedly, I was relieved, both on the personal and professional levels. Caroline continued speaking, and began to talk about her uncle's tendency to tease her about her sexuality, but

[12] For Lacan's critique of the notion that the therapist is in a position to provide such a "corrective emotional experience," or "emotional reeducation" simply by reacting differently than the parent, see Lacan (1961/2002).

[13] This, of course, would allow me to ask, in a somewhat disguised way, "What do you want?"

stopped herself, saying that she felt like she ought not to criticize him. Then, one of her more ambiguous statements:

"I just don't know how certain things can have such an impact on a certain topic. Not just sexuality, but other things."

"What is it that's having an impact?"

"I guess a group of things. One is he just kind of talks about other people a lot."

"Uncle Bob?"

"Yeah. This past week—it made me uncomfortable—this past week he was talking about, like—it's really stupid. This past week it's Miley Cyrus, who's even younger than me, talking about how he saw her boobs online and how great they were."

Here there seemed to be at least a partial answer to some of the questions above. First, the transference was apparent enough to get her talking more freely about her uncle, and not enough to threaten the therapy. I had not crossed the boundary, at least not harmfully. Further, she seemed to be saying that what upset her about Bob was his untamed expression of his own sexual desire in front of her, or his implication of her in it (that is, he often compared Caroline with larger-breasted women). Upon mentioning Miley Cyrus, Caroline became visibly angry, raising her voice somewhat and declaring that her uncle is old enough to be Miley Cyrus's father. Perhaps another hint that this sexual attention was too close for Caroline's comfort? If that were the case, as I imagined it to be, Caroline once again had my countertransferential sympathy. In fact, I was more or less taking it as a given that this was the upshot of her comments.

Yet, once again, Caroline was somewhere other than where I expected her to be. Her next statement, animated with a rare indignation, was this: "I just don't feel comfortable hearing about how he feels about other girls! And in turn, I started to resent Miley Cyrus!" I was reminded that, no matter how compelling our sympathies as clinicians, we must allow ourselves to be surprised by (the Other in) the patient, and follow what she has to say.

"Tell me about that resentment."

"I don't know, it's just … I guess … like … how … come … I … get … so … little … attention."

"Mm hm."

"Or something like that, for something I would do. But her boobs pop out of her shirt and she gets gloated on forever. I guarantee you if I was going around showing my boobs I wouldn't get the same reactions from him! And if you try to say something, he says you're just jealous."

"So when you get upset about it, he says you're jealous that he's not sexually attracted to you? Is that accurate?"

"Kinda. I don't want him to be attracted to me, but pay attention to other stuff that's going on. When he's braggin' about Miley and all the guys she'll get, in a way she is his daughter. And when I ask him how to talk to a guy, he tells me I should try being ditzy."

This fragment of Caroline's discourse provides a concise example of the conflict between the desire for her uncle's love, Bob's desire for Caroline to be sexual in a specific way and Caroline's Oedipal wishes toward Bob as a father figure.

Caroline's dismay at her Uncle Bob's sexualized comments about Miley Cyrus takes a surprising turn here. Her explanation for her anger, far from being what I expected, sounded more like the words of a jealous lover: "I just don't feel comfortable hearing about how he feels about other girls!" She even stated that she had begun to resent the woman competing for her uncle's attention. The same tone is evident in her statement, "I guarantee you if I was going around showing my boobs I wouldn't get the same reactions from him." Both of these comments seem to strongly imply that she would, in fact, want such a reaction from him.

Of course, there is that other dynamic at work here: Caroline's simple desire to be loved as a child would be loved by a parent or caretaker. She states this explicitly: "How come I get so little attention … for something I would do? … I don't want him to be attracted to me, but pay attention to other stuff that's going on."

As discussed previously in my exposition of her two dreams, Caroline's situation seems to be that her desire for Uncle Bob's attention is met with the fact that (in her eyes) the only means of securing his attention would be to become a sexual object. She therefore partially occupies the Oedipal position of desiring to attract him sexually, but only for the sake of embodying his desire. Caroline herself put it this way not long after this session:

"It's not like we spend time or do things together, but I don't think that hurting him or telling him I don't like something he does would help the situation."

"So you'll take what you can get?"

"*I'll take how much I can handle*," she said with an intensity and emotional honesty that I won't soon forget.

Caroline had now begun to discuss her cognizance of the sexual nature of her uncle's attention, as well as her willingness to take that kind of attention (as much as she can "handle") in order to have any attention at all.

Inadvertently, then, by pursuing a question born of my countertransference anxiety surrounding her transference, I was able to elicit from Caroline more speech about the complex relationship she had with Bob. In this instance, she provided a more (if not entirely) conscious articulation of what I had heard in the dreams discussed previously: the desire for her uncle's desire, even if that desire is sexual. The sense that Caroline must capitulate to whatever terms her uncle sets in the relationship is made all the more understandable by the loss of her own father early in life. We see in her discussion of Miley Cyrus again the wish to have a father figure, even if that means putting herself in the position of a sexual object who could have her uncle's child, which resonates with my earlier hypotheses, but the evidence is presented much more consciously. If the point of analytic psychotherapy is to make the unconscious more conscious, then it would seem Caroline had made some progress.

Getting Caught: The Symptomatic Act

During the times her uncle made her sit on his lap, Caroline would generally wait for a predetermined period of time before she removed herself from the immediate situation. She would "watch the clock for 7 to 10 minutes, 'til I think it's acceptable to leave. Longer if he's been in a bad mood." Caroline later brought up another situation in which she tended to wait 10 minutes—this time, not in order to leave her uncle's presence without hurting his feelings, but to wait for a text message back from a man she was interested in. I pointed out to her the connection between this situation and the other by saying "You put a 10-minute limit on it? You put a 10-minute limit on other things too ..." Caroline saw the connection, and mentioned that in both situations she worried about losing the man concerned. During this discussion, however, a behavior that had by now become familiar to me resurfaced with intensity.

In most sessions, Caroline had the presumably nervous habit of making an O-shape with her left hand, while inserting the index finger of her right hand into her left repeatedly. At first glance, this seemed to correlate with her level of anxiety at any given moment, and often increased during her long silences. For the first few months of therapy, I did not comment on this, given the fact that she seemed rather uncomfortable and preoccupied with the possibility of my judging her in the session. I felt that it was better to build a rapport during our first few months than to begin making "process comments" that might only serve to humiliate her and provoke even more anxiety than what she already was feeling.

About four months into the therapy, however, I decided to mention the behavior, since I imagined it was significant as its own kind of speech-act. When I asked an open-ended question, something akin to "what can you tell me about what you're doing with your hands?" She immediately became stock-still ("frozen," as she would become when she would sit on her uncle's lap). She looked away from me, and very slowly produced words to the effect that her mother and uncle had pointed this out to her as well, and that she was afraid I might think it was a "weird" thing to do. I asked her why I might think it is weird, and she explained that "not many people do it, that I've seen." Her apparent embarrassment continued through an extended silence, so I asked how she felt about my pointing this out. She replied: "I feel like you caught me."

"Caught you?"

"Doing something I shouldn't be doing. I feel kind of ashamed of myself for some reason. Like being a kid again, getting caught doing something you're not supposed to be and it gets pointed out in front of everybody."

I asked Caroline for associations concerning what she might have been "caught" doing as a child, and she recalled other children making fun of her during middle school because she showed an interest in a boy. She was unable to come up with any other associations.

Freud (1905a) wrote about what he called "symptomatic acts" in several places, among them the case of Dora:

> I give the name of symptomatic acts to those acts which people perform, as we say, automatically, unconsciously, without attending to them … they are actions to which people would like to deny any significance … these actions, about which consciousness knows nothing or wishes to know nothing, in fact give expression to unconscious thoughts and impulses, and are therefore most valuable and instructive as being manifestations of the unconscious. (p. 76)

During a part of the analysis that Freud hypothesizes is relevant to the issue of childhood masturbation, he tells his patient about his theory. Dora denies that she had ever masturbated as a child, but several days later begins "playing with" a small reticule she is wearing. Freud (1905a) tells us that she kept "opening it, putting a finger into it, shutting it again, and so on" (p. 76). Freud's interpretation is that Dora is indeed masturbating (albeit through a displacement onto the vulva-like reticule) right there in his consulting room, even as she denies ever having masturbated. In other words, Freud tells us, Dora is announcing that she would like to do the very thing she is denying having any experience of.

The reader may have anticipated that I am about to make a similar interpretation of Caroline's behavior. And indeed, one way of making sense of our exchange is to very slightly rephrase what had occurred, without losing any accuracy about the facts of the situation. In asking about what she was doing with her hands, I had effectively pointed out to Caroline that she was touching her own body, and she in turn felt like I had "caught [her] doing something [she was] not supposed to." She connected her sense of shame to an incident in which she had showed a kind of erotic desire (her attraction to a boy in her adolescence), and she noted that "not many people do it, that I've seen." This last statement is generally true of masturbation, which tends to remain hidden from the view of others and is often stigmatized by children, who internalize the views of their parents. All that was missing was the statement of the thing itself, the word "masturbation." The rest of the discourse around this behavior, and indeed the behavior itself (qua discourse), seemed to be speaking clearly. This, as I have mentioned, was quite characteristic of Caroline's therapy. There were many moments when she had all but stated something outright, but then came across as being nowhere near conscious of what seemed to me like the obvious missing piece. Now, Caroline's ego was once again absent exactly where I expected her to be present.[14]

The more important question may have been why this behavior increased when it did, and why she expressed her feelings of being caught at that particular time. The matter being discussed when

[14] In fact, I did point out to Caroline that her feeling of being caught and the example she provided seemed to have a certain resonance with sexual desire. That is, this exchange occurred when we were discussing her romantic interest in a boy, and she connected her feeling of being caught to having been caught experiencing erotic feelings for a boy years ago. I wondered aloud if there was something in her experience about being caught having a sexual desire. I did not at this time voice my impression of the symptomatic masturbatory act, since it seemed this would only enact exactly what her transference had set up: an authoritarian Other actually catching her masturbating and "pointing it out." This, given both the theory of hysterical discourse I discussed previously and my session-to-session experience with Caroline, was only likely to engage her in the project of disavowing the interpretation, and going to some lengths to show that I had been wrong (therefore attempting to frustrate what she might have taken to be my desire that she conform to my interpretation). This tentative interpretation may have laid the groundwork for her comments in the next session regarding her uncle's attention to other women (see the following text).

Caroline began her "symptomatic act" was her experience with her would-be boyfriend, who seemed to ignore her text messages. She was commenting on the fact that she would wait 10 minutes before trying a second time to elicit a reply from the now twice-as-absent man. We had connected this to the 10 minutes that she would wait before leaving her uncle's full-body embrace when she began fidgeting with her hands. Therefore, with only one degree of remove, this apparently displaced masturbatory behavior, along with her feeling of having been caught, was situated within the context of sitting on her Uncle Bob's lap. Why would this context have elicited this kind of embodied speech? I will return to this question later.

This was not the only moment in therapy when there seemed to be a strong elicitation of masturbation, via both Caroline's bodily actions and her speech. Remarkably, they often occurred in the context of her mentioning the 10-minute waiting period. Caroline had by then implemented this waiting period in therapy as well. She would often wait precisely 10 minutes before speaking in therapy or sometimes between comments (without consciously gauging her time, as far as I could tell). Therefore, the 10-minute waiting period was a somewhat frequent point of reference for her, after I had once pointed out that she had waited silently for that period of time. One of the several examples of this occurred about 6 months after the session I've just described:

"Maybe you're quiet to see if I speak in 10-minute intervals. 'Cause I have that 10-minute thing. Maybe it's genetically encoded. I also feel like by being quiet I'm doing something I'm not supposed to be doing."

"Something you're not supposed to be doing?"

"Yeah. I guess I'm slackin'"

"What does slackin' mean?"

"Same thing, I guess. Not fulfilling your purpose to the extent that you should be."

"Slackin' off?"

"Exactly."

"So, slackin' off is something you're not supposed to be doing."

Caroline suddenly looked angry, and raised her voice as she said, "No! Well, it's *not*! It's something you should *never* do, because you're doing half the job of it! You can do something and ... and still ... I guess just not do it the way it should be done, or ... you just show up and not do what you're supposed to do. But I guess there are some differences between what I just said and what I'm doing. I showed up, and I'm trying to make the effort and there's still no results."

Once again, we see the phrase "doing something I'm not supposed to be doing." The rest of the dialogue (and its continuation not printed here) indicated that Caroline might have intended to describe her silence as "not doing something I'm supposed to be doing" rather than "doing something I'm not supposed to be doing." Caroline felt frustrated with the fact that she was not speaking enough for the therapeutic context, and felt as though she was "slackin' off" by virtue of that. But what she actually said was "I'm doing something I'm not supposed to be doing." This change in the position of "not" in the sentence makes the utterance seem to reference the earlier session in which she had felt "caught" by me. It also occurred in the same context—while the subject of the 10-minute silence was thematic. Given my impressions in the earlier and subsequent sessions, I wondered whether her comments may have been unconsciously related to this issue of masturbation.

Caroline then elaborated on the "something [she is] not supposed to be doing" as "slackin,'" which I took up as "slackin' off," a commonly used version of the slang phrase. This signifier is sonically similar to "jacking off," and "whacking off." Further, it echoes her phrase "smacking off trees," which she used in her description of her dream about wolves entering her yard, which seemed to have its own connections to sexuality and masturbation (see previous discussion). And like the session in which she described feeling "caught," she had a poverty of associations to her peculiar phrase.

The sudden affective charge in her speech is also of some importance here. Upon my repetition: "So, slackin' off is something you're not supposed to be doing," Caroline suddenly became very animated in her response that it was not indeed—an emphasis that seemed to carry the weight of a serious moral injunction (as taboos against masturbation and sexual behaviors generally often are). Her description of the reasons for the unacceptability of "slackin' off" can be taken as yet more evidence for this interpretation. Caroline's concern was that slackin' off is only "doing half the job of it," which is precisely the critique of masturbation provided by the Christianity in which Caroline was raised: that masturbation is sinful because it involves only one person in an activity in which there "ought" to be two people coming together for the purpose of reproduction. It is pleasure without reproduction: "half the job." It also involves only half the people necessary to do the "complete" job.

At this point I felt that it was practicable to make a somewhat more explicit interpretation than I had 6 months earlier. The therapeutic alliance was much more solidly established, other gains had been made in therapy, and the fullness of her discourse with the latent meanings I had been hearing seemed to have come to an optimal point. Repeating back to her some of the phrases she had just used, I asked her (with what I hoped was a bit of tact) if they seemed like they might apply to masturbation and parental attitudes about it. Surprisingly, there was almost no silence, and Caroline replied easily[15] "I guess there's a duality about it. I was brought up one way, then there's culture."

"How were you brought up?"

"Marriage before sex, you know."

Since this exchange had begun by talking about masturbation explicitly, I asked, "And that it's wrong to masturbate? (Here the reader may notice a bit more force than I have presented in my interventions throughout this book. Such moments were relatively

[15] Perhaps an example of how the therapist's hesitation or discomfort with given subject matter—in this case, my own fear of hurting Caroline by discussing sexuality (see previous discussion)—might be misguided. I assumed that this subject was a dangerous one, but Caroline engaged it easily.

rare. However, I felt that my insistence on staying on topic here was justified because of the proximity I sensed to the latent subject matter here, combined with my confidence that Caroline's investment in the therapy and the therapeutic relationship was sufficient to withstand a bit of such force. Here, as opposed to earlier in the therapy, I could afford to push Caroline to be present to her discourse in ways that might be uncomfortable.)

"Yeah, and I guess that conflicts with everything else."

This led into a discussion of the messages she received from her family about the taboo of sexual pleasure, especially for women, versus the attitude of her uncle: that she was to be a sexual object for him and other men. Once again, in the context of the 10-minute silence in her uncle's (and by extension, other men's) presence, allusions to masturbation seemed present in Caroline's speech. This time, I made the interpretation explicitly, which led Caroline to discuss the impasse at which she found herself vis-à-vis her uncle, her sexuality, and her desire in general—the three elements that formed the nexus that had not admitted much discussion at the beginning of therapy, and which I felt was essential to Caroline's progress.

A Memory

The themes that I have been discussing here—Caroline's desire in general and as present in sexuality, the issue of masturbation, her cognizance of the sexualized nature of her uncle's attention, and her complicity in that sexualized attention (as she incarnates the desire of the Other)—have all been introduced by way of linguistically based extrapolations on my part that may have struck the reader as more than a little fanciful at times. I've attempted to show through careful citation of the data of Caroline's speech my basis for making such interpretations, but as in Chapter 5, there has so far been little conscious speech from Caroline that bears out my hypotheses. The reader may appropriately remind me that the therapist is never immune from Lacan's doctrine of *méconnaisance*, the misrecognition or misunderstanding of the other person's speech and action—and that this is especially the case here.

It is hard *not* to recognize the danger here, that the aspects of my formulation of the case that I have discussed in this chapter may have been no more than hackneyed psychoanalytic fabrications that bore more relevance to my own theoretical interests or even prurient interest than to the important issues that Caroline brought to therapy. I struggled a great deal with the question of the viability of these interpretations myself throughout most of the therapy, and I continue to be aware of how much I may sound like I am trying to re-create Dora, having cast myself as the no-longer-inimitable Dr. Freud. But the memory I am about to discuss helped impart some confidence that, as suspect as they may sound, these aspects of my formulation had in fact been useful.

A central question that had remained unanswered during almost the entire year of therapy was that of why Caroline's specific brand of fidgeting, as well as language that seemed connected to masturbation surfaced at times when she had been discussing the period of 10 minutes of silence while her uncle set her on his lap, holding her from behind. So far in the therapy, there had been no real explanation for this connection.

Further, the question remained as to why, even if the above interpretations of her dreams are correct on this count, Caroline made an unconscious connection between her own "castration" and her uncle's ability to have sexual enjoyment. While it is theoretically characteristic of the hysteric to feel that she must foreclose on her own desire in order to embody the Other's desire, to simply cite this convention would be to beg the fundamental question: Where did that structure come from? It is traditionally offered in psychoanalytic thinking that the girl sees that the father has a penis and she has none, thereby concluding that men are the only ones capable of sexual pleasure, a notion that is culturally reinforced. But in Caroline's case, it seemed that the fantasy upon which she operated was that she had to be castrated (without agency, without desire) *in order for* her uncle to have pleasure or to be attracted to her. Similarly, Caroline felt that it would drive her uncle away from her if she wanted anything beyond him—her own living situation, her own career plans, even her own space away from his embrace—and she was terrified by the idea of hurting him with her own desire. Why?

At the end of therapy, a memory surfaced for Caroline. This memory not only seemed to substantiate my interpretive hypotheses to some extent, but also addressed the questions I've just raised. While I emphatically do *not* mean to suggest that such complex dynamics (the surface of which I have only scratched in this chapter) can be traced back to one single memory, the anamnesis of which will furnish a cure, as Freud postulated in his early work with hysterics, I do agree that they may hold some therapeutic value, whether they correspond to one particular memory or a consolidation of memories, or even if they are only accurate representations of an unconscious fantasy that fuels the patient's symptoms.

Caroline recalled the following in one of her last sessions:

"I was little. Three or four. I remember sitting on his lap on the chair when I was little and him telling me what I was doing wasn't nice. But I just wasn't ready for bed, and I was bored and I couldn't get up, and Uncle Bob was there, holding me, and I was trying to amuse myself somehow. And he just freaked out. He just yelled and said things about how I was a bad kid. And he smacked me. I don't remember much after the fact."[16]

Beyond providing additional evidence for the hypothesis that Caroline's often painful habit of jamming her finger into her fist was a "symptomatic act" that alluded to masturbation, this recollection gives us a sense of *why* such behavior would often occur in connection with her discussions (and, at times, enactments in therapy) of the "10-minute silence" with which she responded to her uncle's embrace. According to this memory, which turned

[16] Caroline confirmed that the means of "amusing [her]self" which wasn't appropriate was in fact masturbation.

out to be the earliest she had of her uncle setting her on his lap (contradicting what she had reported earlier, that these scenes had begun in adolescence) masturbation was something she did to amuse herself while he did so. We also find here a possible answer to the question of why Caroline felt that I had "caught" her doing something she was "not supposed to do" when I asked her about the behavior.

Similarly, her lack of a conscious experience of sexual desire, which I met with the (silent) tentative theory that she felt that she had to be castrated in order for her uncle to have sexual pleasure (as per the two dreams discussed earlier in this chapter) is addressed by this memory. She touched her genitals, and was told it was not nice—by the man who was taking pleasure in cuddling with her during the act. A reasonable conclusion for the young Caroline to have drawn might be that her own physical or sexual pleasure (the satisfaction of her own desire) would interfere with her uncle's desire to hold her. This goes beyond simply feeling that Bob's approval depended upon her negation of her own sexual desire, and her becoming simply a means of attracting men (to reproduce). Rather, his pleasure, and consequently his desire for her depended upon it. In her view, then, he needed her to become an object for the pleasure of the Other, without sexual desire or pleasure of her own. We might, given the fact that we know Caroline saw her uncle as only able to approve of women as sexual objects, surmise that Caroline felt that his approval depended upon her ability to make him want to hold her—that his pleasure with her was a prerequisite for his approval.

BECOMING CURIOUS ABOUT DESIRE

It would seem, then, that the series of interpretive misunderstandings of Caroline's language and actions that I pursued had some basis in her psychological reality. This came as a bit of a surprise to me, since despite the fact that I enjoy this kind of hypothesizing, I remained skeptical of its relevance to the person I was working with. As I mentioned, these hypotheses seem so classical that they can't be reasonable. But the question of accuracy aside, perhaps a better test to apply to such misunderstandings is whether they are *useful to the project of therapy.* Did they allow the clinician to help direct the patient to a position from which she could engage thoughts, memories, fantasies, feelings, and wishes in ways that helped her to grow beyond the impasse she was in at the beginning of treatment?

In Caroline's case, they seemed to. Of course, as with any purely psychotherapeutic intervention, we are left without objective, compelling, scientific evidence that it was my pursuit of this particular set of latent meanings in Caroline's speech that had this effect. But this is a larger problem that plagues any research into psychotherapy. The fact remains that this was the style of intervention that I chose, and Caroline experienced some change during our time together. This change was not as concrete as some other patients experience; that is, Caroline did not make any major changes in her life that I know of while we worked together. But she did seem to change psychologically. While there was a great deal more involved in the therapy than I am presenting here, I will comment briefly on some of that change.

First, she became capable of thinking about and discussing aloud the sexual overtones in her uncle's behavior toward her, and began to name them as such. The reader will recall that, at first, there was a gap in her narration of her uncle's habits, comparing her sexually to other women, and other related behaviors. As we pursued what was latent in her discourse via the method of following the letter, which I've attempted to describe here, Caroline began to speak more explicitly about what she called the "dynamic." This, in turn, produced the result that she was able to have discussions that did not paint her uncle (nor herself, at times) in the most flattering light without becoming overwhelmed by guilt and anxiety, feelings that constituted two of her major clinical complaints.

Secondly, Caroline began to talk more about disentangling her desire from that of her uncle. She began to sharply question whether the career she was pursuing was simply for Bob's sake, and consequently whether she needed to devote her professional life to being what he desired. Perhaps more importantly, and more foundationally, Caroline became aware of the fact that her desire, sexuality, and her relationship with her uncle were intimately connected with one another in the first place. She made this realization *of her own accord*, without relying upon any interpretation I had made. Rather, I believe the stage had been set for her in the way I pursued her speech to make that connection for herself.

More generally, Caroline began to talk about her relationship to desire itself, which was perhaps the most taboo subject in her early discourse. The question of what she wanted often seemed utterly alien, rarely surfacing in her commentary, and when I would ask explicitly about it, I was often met with stunned silence or confusion. This, of course, was the centerpiece of the therapy, and here we return to the theoretical question with which we began the chapter: How do we bring the hysteric back to her own desire? How do we ask her "What do you want?" in such a way that she becomes engaged in the project of finding out?

In the case of this therapy, the method I've discussed here did not bring Caroline to a conclusive answer to that question. However, I believe that Caroline did begin to engage the question more deeply than she had in the past. She began to find some words to talk about desire toward the end of our year together, and described to me a recurring feeling of *wanting*. The feeling was not necessarily new, but her ability to discuss it and interrogate it was. This wanting had no particular object, and she sometimes mistook it for a desire for food, being quickly disappointed to find out that food was not this desire's object. Perhaps the desire had no object. What is important from my perspective, however, was that it was *her* desire, and she could disentangle herself enough from the desire of the Other to admit to having it. Further, in discussing this, she knew that she was satisfying my desire for her to talk about her own desire, which marked a departure from the usual hysterical maintenance of an unsatisfied desire in the Other. It may be argued that this was achieved via not naming the object of her desire, and perhaps rightfully so. But it also may be that this was a beginning for Caroline, a major step toward finding out something more about what she wanted. More importantly, she began to *want to know what that was.*

LACAN AND RELATIONAL THINKING

With Caroline, we face a predicament familiar to therapists of all stripes—that of how to effectively relate to and treat the patient who seems to disown much of her own subjectivity and desire (even at times her desire to be in therapy or to speak to the therapist). My wager here is that this thorny problem can be elucidated by Lacanian structural diagnostic theory. Here, I've brought in the work of Fink and Soler in this regard, as the primary source material is, at the time of this writing, still untranslated. Their commentary illustrates the problem that a Lacanian orientation poses when considering the position of the "hysteric" in psychotherapy, especially in relation to the therapist. That is, how is the therapist, who operates largely upon the desire for the patient to speak, to deal effectively with a patient whose habit it is to first divine and then frustrate the desire of the Other? How are we to get a patient to consider what it is she wants, when it will be counterproductive to show that we want her to do so? I have tried to illustrate here the way in which attention to the letter of the patient's speech can be an integral part of the project of helping this to happen.

Other clinicians (see Fink, 1997; Goldman, 2004) have written about hysterical structure vis-à-vis the patient's own life outside therapy, and Goldman (2004) has discussed hysterical structure in play in the therapeutic relationship inasmuch as the patient's transference recapitulates relationships with those outside the therapy setting. In our discussion of Caroline, however, I have tried to make a more in-depth exploration of some of what was specifically at stake in my own countertransference than has been done previously in Lacanian clinical literature. Furthermore, I am staking out the position, alongside those of the relational school, that countertransference can be informative and helpful to clinical work (even Lacanian clinical work) but that it is not helpful *in itself*, and must rather be interrogated from the point of view of the clinician's understanding of how the countertransferential fantasy will impact the case—whether it will serve to free the patient's speech or to stunt it, subordinating it to the therapist's drive for narcissistic gratification. I advocate using countertransference as an instrument that helps to *regulate* the possibility of the therapist to make therapy about himself, rather than as an opportunity to make therapy more about himself, and thereby somehow furnish a cure to the patient, as advocated by Davies (2004), Renik (1999), Maroda (1999, 2001), and others. Perhaps this represents a new step in dialogue between relational thinking and Lacanian thinking.

Caroline's case also underscores the explicit link between the presence of a *thought* that unconsciously manifests itself in much of the patient's language (in this case, Caroline's memory of masturbating on the chair with her uncle, and being punished) and the *characterological tendencies* of that patient (in Caroline's case, her need to renounce her own desire and pleasure in order to maintain her position as that which the Other desires). Caroline helps us see how attention to the peculiarities and double meanings in a patient's language can yield important anamnestic results, which it is generally agreed in psychodynamic and psychoanalytic therapy can have the result of setting a process of psychological and characterological change in motion.

HOLES

There are, of course, gaps here. As with Jim, Eric, and Steve, I have left out discussion of much of the work that I consider foundational to psychotherapy: the creation of a strong therapeutic alliance, for example, and the maintenance of the therapeutic frame. It is arguable, then, that Caroline's progress in beginning to realize that her desire was caught up with sexuality, and that both were connected to her uncle, was due not to my pursuit of the letter of her speech, but to the relational processes that I attended to as part of the background of therapy.[17] One example of this, which I did here, was my decision to inquire about whether I had crossed a boundary in asking a sexually oriented question of Caroline. She responded that there was a difference in the way I had approached the subject and the way in which it was approached at home. Following the theory of the corrective emotional experience, and the relational school's thoughts on the healing power of the therapeutic relationship, it may have been moments such as these (of which there were many) that held the real therapeutic power.

And I may have grossly misinterpreted a number of moments in the therapy as great successes when they were anything but. For example, in my discussion of Caroline's response to my question: "So, slackin' off is something you're not supposed to be doing?" (To which she responded with an emphatic "No!") I interpreted her burst of affect as a sign that I had hit upon important, psychologically charged material. It may just as well be that I had simply annoyed her. That is, it was quite plain to hear that Caroline had meant that "slackin' off" was something she was not supposed to be doing, and my habit of playing dumb by asking questions that had obvious answers may have provoked her to raise her voice. I may have mistaken simple annoyance with my therapeutic style as evidence of its efficaciousness!

Further, even within the framework of a Lacanian-informed practice, there is the very real danger that the classicist frame of my interpretive speculations about Caroline's material narrowed the scope of what I was able to hear in the letter of her speech. As I noted above, the way in which some of the imagery in Caroline's dreams seemed to lend itself so readily to clichéd Freudian "interpretations" involving phallic symbols and castration did not

---

[17] Of course, I would argue that attention to the letter of speech is in fact a relational process—with the Other, as I did in the case of Jim.

escape my attention, and it may be that my attention refused to let these ideas escape, until I finally discovered what I had decided to see from the beginning. Caroline may well have simply read my desire, despite my attempts to focus upon hers, and simply furnished me with hints and fragments of what she realized I wanted to hear—thus making the progress I thought I was seeing look like nothing of the sort, but rather a simple repetition of her usual pattern of becoming the object of desire for the Other. It is difficult to know whether this was in fact the case, and the question remains one "hole" among others in this case study.

But it may also be that we are at times slightly too eager to dismiss ideas that sound too Freudian out of an almost phobic response: a response, it is true, to an analytic tradition of narcissism, of the too-simple answers that tie themselves to intellectual rigidity, of misogyny, and of sexual obsession.

And we often tell ourselves that, in the age of YouTube, sexting, and reality television, our society has become so liberalized, so sexually disinhibited, that the effects of sexual taboo are no longer relevant, even if they were in Freud's day.

But Freud's ideas regarding repression and sexual taboo cannot be entirely reduced to the analytic culture in this country that came to adopt them. And the fact of large-scale sexual disinhibition does not preclude the possibility of sexual trauma. In fact, it may make it all the more relevant. Consider Caroline's uncle, and his highly "liberated" enjoyment of the sexuality of celebrities, and his "open-mindedness" in sharing these pleasures with his niece.

Many patients struggle, in this very day and age, with pain that organizes itself around taboo and trauma, and we will not serve them well by refusing to approach these issues in order to distance ourselves from the mistakes of our psychoanalytic forbears.

7

Conclusions

I am not, where I am the plaything of my thought …

—Lacan (1957/2002, p. 517)

This book set out to explore what a therapist's attunement to the letter of the patient's language, as advocated in the writings of Jacques Lacan, might mean in the context of American psychotherapy. More specifically, I attempted to show ways in which attention to the letter of patients' speech about symptoms, memories, fantasies, dreams, and the therapeutic relationship affected my case formulations, interventions, and the general direction of the psychotherapies in question. This is a response to a paucity of detailed clinical research illustrating the practical implementation of such an approach, especially within the more mainstream psychodynamic therapeutic frame, with patients who were not already well-versed in psychoanalysis or Lacanian theory.

Can Lacan's conception of language be practical for a psychotherapist practicing in the real world? And if so, how? Although this kind of inquiry may have rankled Lacan himself, whom we might imagine being dismissive of the pedestrian nature of such an American, pragmatic question, I believe it warrants investigation if we grant that Lacan should have any place on the American clinical scene, which is more and more dominated by pragmatic interests.

To that end, I believe Jim, Eric, Steve, and Caroline have shown us, in a limited way, that Lacanian theory and technique are *learnable* and *useful* to the larger therapeutic venture.

THE COURSE OF FOUR TREATMENTS

By now, it is clear to the reader that case conceptualization is a driving force in this book, as it is in my approach to therapy generally. I believe case conceptualization has become quite undervalued in favor of the increasingly popular notion of "doing what works" to get symptom reduction in our patients. It is more difficult than we often make it sound to differentiate conceptualization from intervention. Here, I have tried to demonstrate detailed and cogent case conceptualization based upon the patient's speech *to the letter*, and to focus on the blurry line between conceptualization and intervention, where much of our best work occurs.

Lacanian conceptualization and intervention proceed from the *readily observable* phenomena of the language the patient uses. Lacan's "Seminar on 'The Purloined Letter'" (1966/2006) was taken up in Chapter 3 in order to show that, despite a reputation for obscurantism, we can view Lacan's writings as encouraging the clinician to begin with what she sees and hears, rather than with constructs that make conjectures about what cannot be seen but *should* be found. That is, Lacan encourages clinicians to take a lesson from Poe's detective Dupin, and attend first to the obvious: the patient's words. Lacan suggests that the unconscious functions via the displacement of signifiers rather than the burial of affect, and that this fact makes the unconscious a more accessible phenomenon than we might think.

Jim, who complained of being "stuck" in his life, ruminated about not being "productive" enough for himself and the women in his life, and suffered from terrifying, intrusive thoughts in bathrooms. We discovered that Jim's significations about a variety of issues were applicable—when taken at the level of the words themselves rather than their intended meaning—to excretion. I adopted the assumption that if these odd features of Jim's language were of any therapeutic value, they must demonstrate themselves to be so via Jim's own process of discovery, and not by my forceful interpretation. So I attempted, per Lacanian theory (especially as re-presented by Bruce Fink) to simply punctuate these curious turns of phrase by repetition, facial responses, or ambiguous sounds like "mm hmm" in order to draw Jim's attention to them, even if subtly.

The result was that Jim began "producing" a steadily increasing number of such polyvalent signifiers, all of which could be applied to urination and defecation. Finally, Jim began to connect his habit of "withholding" his feelings and thoughts from the women in his life and the traumatic events around an episode of constipation during his childhood. The emergence of this memory (which played a major role in the remainder of Jim's therapy) was arguably partially or even directly a result of the linguistically based approach I took to this case. Jim's connection of this childhood event to his current symptoms was his *own*, and although it coincided with my case formulation, did not rely on an interpretation I made, which perhaps made it all the more valuable to Jim.

What about affect? It is often a critique of Lacanian clinical work that it neglects affect, but this instance reminds us that this need not be the case. The connections between signifiers that Jim had begun to make actually resulted in *heightened affective experience* and not just an intellectualized approach to his problems. He also began to develop a new, more affectively dynamic, outlook on his relationship with his mother. Clinical attention to language should not result in constricted affect, but rather greater freedom to experience an affective range, which was heretofore inaccessible due to the patient's constricted ability to speak his subjectivity. Jim's therapy shows that affective goals of mainstream psychodynamic therapy are not anathema to a Lacanian approach, but that there may be a disagreement as to the best means of achieving a genuine affective range in our patients. I argued that the broadening of the patient's affective range should not be based upon a "black box" of repressed emotion[1] as imagined by the clinician, but should proceed from careful scrutiny of the patient's own discourse. By showing the way in which I attempted such scrutiny, I hope to have provided a somewhat clear picture of an alternative means to attain the broadening of affective experience, as well as opening up the potential for more depth and breadth within the patient's therapeutic discourse.

Lacan's "Seminar on 'The Purloined Letter'" has not, to my knowledge, been put into dialogue with specific clinical material as of the time of this writing, and it is in hopes of evaluating the usefulness of Lacan's writings in contemporary American psychotherapy that I have done so here.

Along these same lines, my discussion of this seminar in a clinical context also served to bring Lacan into dialogue with other psychological thinkers. We cannot discount, as zealots might, the possible harmony between Lacan's thinking and that of those whom he has elsewhere criticized, for example, thinkers who proposed an existential psychology such as Sartre, who sought to critique psychoanalysis by virtue of its top-heavy constructs (Lacan, 1949/2002, p. 8). By implication, we might also consider the work of Laing, Heidegger, and Boss to occupy this common ground as well.

"The Function and Field of Speech and Language in Psychoanalysis" (1953/2002) affords us a view of Lacan's radical stance against the notion of a hard-to-define interpersonal "contact" in the "two-body" or "two-person" psychology proposed by Balint, and more recently taken up by the relational school. What, then, are we to do with the demands made of us by the therapeutic relationship? Whether it is a question of transference, countertransference, resistance, love, or aggression, no viable therapeutic approach can afford to ignore the exigencies of the relationship at hand. In each of the preceding case studies, I have attempted to show that a Lacanian approach need not ignore the therapeutic

[1] Repressed emotion being a concept to which Lacan did not subscribe, and which he claimed Freud never posited.

relationship, and that even when we constrict our discussion to the way in which we work with the patient's language, we find viable means of approaching that relationship therapeutically.

Although all of these case studies speak to the relationship in one way or another, I discussed it directly and at length in Chapter 4. My attempt at a detailed theoretical examination of Lacan's "Aggressiveness in Psychoanalysis" (1953/2002; an essay rarely commented upon theoretically, and never commented upon clinically), was meant to explore the way in which the character and content of the therapeutic relationship can be used clinically via engagement of the symbolic register of the patient's psychological life. We can make the case that this approach to an apparently aggressive act yields therapeutic material that is richer than what might result from the client simply "swallowing" (to borrow some Kleinian terminology) an interpretation made by the therapist. This opening-up of what Winnicott (1971) might call "potential space" in Eric's discourse became part of a larger therapeutic process of Eric's seeing that there may be more to his psychological life than he had previously known.

Of course, the relationship is bound up with the transference, and Eric's speech in session, memories, and dreams to help us approach that as well. Through attending to the letter in Eric's dreams, we gained a greater understanding of his transference feelings and thoughts, as well as his wishes and anxieties about the project of therapy itself. One example of this is our analysis of the sentence generated by one dream, "I relieved myself in a Formica drawer," which yielded, via close attention to the letter, the statement, "I revealed myself as a reward for Michael," a key fantasy in Eric's approach to therapy, which in turn clarified our understanding of Eric's approach to living. My hope is that Chapter 4 yields some ideas about how to attend to transference, and to the therapeutic relationship, without eclipsing the patient's subjectivity with that of the therapist.

Power is always at issue in psychotherapy. Numerous theoreticians and practitioners from the highly seasoned to the first-year graduate student have grappled with the problem of therapeutic power relations. Part of what attracts me to Lacan is his concern about the possible, or even likely, abuse of power that occurs when we attempt to "model" health for a patient, and end up engaging in a (sometimes) subtle Pygmalion project. Lacan's critique of the narcissistic tendency in behaviorism no less than psychoanalysis to set out to create a new "ego" for the patient, one that more closely matches that of the therapist, is powerful and relevant.

Yet to attend to language is not to somehow exempt oneself from this problem. It is possible to express approval and disapproval, interest and boredom with an "mm hmm" just as much as we can with more elaborate language. We also presume a certain relationship to the patient vis-à-vis power when we decide to respond to her in ways that are not socially normative, such as punctuating speech or withholding personal information. More to the point, when we choose to draw attention to a given speech act, how are we so sure that it contains within it the potential to find out some greater truth about the patient? Who are we to decide that an apparent accident of language has more to offer than that which the patient is consciously trying to tell us? I am far from original in suggesting that *we never allow ourselves to reify any of our theoretical constructs*, to remember always that what we are doing is to some extent absurd, and to let go of the notion that there is some crystalline truth hidden in a slip of the tongue. I advise that the clinician treat such linguistic events simply as opportunities for the patient to talk more. This attitude has the added benefit of allowing us to be surprised when our formulations are borne out, and helps us not to force upon the patient our attachment to them.

It is also possible for the therapist to set himself up as an authority upon "proper" language, and put the patient in an inferior position based upon class, ethnicity, education type, or home region. I offered a few possible ways of taking up this question. Perhaps most important is the suggestion to approach irregularities in the patient's speech not necessarily as objective indicators of unconscious and disguised thoughts, but as opportunities that the clinician can seize upon to reorient his own attunement to possible meanings and connections that he may not normally notice. It therefore may not be so important that the clinician picks up on a grammatical mistake, for example, as it is that he notices the polyvalence in the patient's speech at all, and grammatical irregularities are one means of doing so. This view allows for a greater sense of the clinician's own subjectivity, which some critics of classical and Lacanian psychoanalysis have pointed out is often strangely absent from its theoretical discourse.

"*Organa Non Grata*" brought our attention, with Steve's help, to another, highly contentious, area of Lacanian theory: the notion of the phallus. I tried to show the way in which the therapy allowed Steve to explore a fundamental loss in childhood (that of the legitimacy of the genitals as part of the person), albeit possibly an indirect and semiconscious exploration. My hope is that I was able to make somewhat clear the way Lacan's notions of the phallus, castration, and the symbolic phallus can be of use to us in understanding the unconscious struggles that pervade psychotherapy, as well as their direct relation to the painful and traumatic losses that are entailed in growing up. The chapter tried to chronicle my attempts to gain access to these struggles by means of following the letter of Steve's speech. During the process of symbolizing his phallic loss, Steve became more able to speak about his sexuality and sexual issues in general, which included his ambivalence about the notion of "a real man."

More important, perhaps, is the fact that for Steve, loss (the loss that emerges "from the residue of an obliteration") (Lacan, 1958/2002), individuality, power, agency, and the phallus were all bound up in each other, and that it is difficult if not impossible to assign temporal or causal primacy to the physical phallus, even as it becomes an important aspect of the therapy. I see this not as a failure of the psychoanalytic emphasis on the phallus so much as further evidence for Lacan and Fink's claim, contra Butler, that the phallus is not reducible to the penis.

As far as I'm aware, Chapter 5 also includes the first occasion of Lacan being put into dialogue with the mainstream American psychodynamic theorist, Harriet Lerner, and her notion of the misnaming of genitalia. This chapter also implied a connection between Lacan and the self psychology influenced Alice Miller, and even Carl Rogers, both of whom focus upon the conditionality of parental acceptance of the child as central to the development of later pathology. Despite the theoretical distance between them, Lacan's notion of the phallus implies common ground between Lacan, Miller, and Rogers, which in turn implies an accessibility and applicability of Lacan for the American clinician.

Chapter 6 explored the question of hysterical desire, and speculated about its genesis and perpetuation in the case of Caroline. Continuing the theme of castration, and using attention to the letter of her speech, we see the traumatic loss of legitimacy of sexual desire early in Caroline's childhood. This chapter was also an attempt to chronicle a clinical situation that is likely familiar to the student of psychotherapy: an encounter with a patient whose desire is notably elusive, whose problems are also elusive, and who seems to make a practice of being elusive to the therapist generally. This is sometimes experienced by the therapist as frustrating, since he quickly finds that it is nigh-impossible to find something he can offer that she will take. Such situations are all the more vexing since they often arise in people whose psychological pain is so great, and whom we feel called to help even as they push us away. Caroline was one such person, and the seriousness of her struggle might be summed up in the quote I used as the epigraph to the chapter: "I just have to be what [my uncle] wants me to be."

What does Lacan—not a little elusive himself—have to offer us in this regard? Not unexpectedly, we garner from Soler and Lacan that the clinician is to help the hysterical subject come into ownership of her desire, whereas her tendency is to discover the desire of the clinician (or the Other) in order to maintain it as unsatisfied. Chapter 6 is an account of my attempt to use the letter of her speech in order to bring her closer to her own desire, for as Lacan

(1958/2002) says, "desire must be taken literally." This chapter once again shows the way in which following signifiers, often by means of free associations, helped me to gain a sophisticated sense of Caroline's struggles and the locus of her missing desire. Like my work with Steve, much of what I began to see emerging in this therapy was related to a sense of castration, and of the problematic nature of sexuality in the sphere of the family, in which it became for Caroline both everything and nothing—both overwhelmingly present and oddly absent.

By following the letter of her discourse—especially that which came up in relation to her dreams—I was able to encourage Caroline to speak more freely about her perception of her uncle's demands, the sexual nature of which had previously gone unnamed by her. It is my contention that following her language in this way ultimately allowed her to begin to voice her *own* complex desires vis-à-vis her Uncle Bob as well as her sexuality, and indeed to begin to differentiate a number of subtle thoughts and feelings that had heretofore been repressed and displaced, thereby driving some of her symptoms. My hope is that by chronicling some of my interventions and including the reader in the process of clinical formulations based on the play of the signifier, I have provided a somewhat "Lacanian" way of approaching those patients whose elusiveness often proves a serious obstacle to continued therapy.

I devoted a part of the discussion in Chapter 6 to my own countertransference, and offer a means of making it useful to the therapy in a way that may be different from the currently fashionable ideas of the relational school, specifically the suggestions of Davies (2004), Maroda (1999), and Renik (1999), that we disclose and give vent to our countertransference thoughts and feelings in order to help heal the patient. I tried to make the point that it may not be out of step with Lacanian theory to see our countertransference as a source of good information, but that it may be best to examine it for what can be useful to the patient before we engage it in any way. I took my own countertransferential response as a point of departure for further questioning of what Caroline needed from therapy at that time, rather than as an edict about what I should or should not do or a pronouncement about her character. The letter of Caroline's speech helped me to situate this point of departure. From this standpoint, I attempted to illustrate that countertransference can be used in a way that is consonant with Lacan's oft-repeated mandate to respect the subjectivity of our patients.

While countertransference has become the subject of much discussion in the era of two-person approaches to psychoanalytic therapy, and the therapeutic relationship has become central to American psychotherapy influenced by existentialism and humanism, it is often absent from clinical discussions of Lacanian psychoanalysis, which are themselves rare. In my experience in the clinical community, Lacan is sometimes regarded as encouraging a lack of attention to countertransference. Although some may indeed take Lacan this way, I do not, and my discussion of Caroline's case attempted to show how one can make Lacanian use of one's countertransference and subjectivity within the therapy. I believe more thinking and dialogue is called for on this subject.

A WORD ON THE FUTURE

Research on the clinical application of Lacanian theory is still in its infancy, and much has yet to be done. Opportunities in qualitative as well as quantitative work abound for researchers who are willing to undertake them.

A patient once asked me whether I ever wondered what happened to my former patients, whether they were well, what they were doing. Of course I do! We all do. If we are honest with ourselves, we must wonder about the viability of our methods as well. As much as I have serious problems with many of the assumptions and attitudes surrounding current forms of efficacy research, we must allow for its potential, in some form anyway, to yield results that benefit patients and clinicians alike.

Recently, mainstream psychological research has begun to produce empirical support for psychoanalytic and psychodynamic therapy (see Leichsenring & Rabun, 2008; Shedler, 2010). The evidence has included randomized controlled trials (RCTs) as well as *in-vivo* studies, and has focused on the fact that psychodynamic therapy tends to be efficacious with complex psychological complaints as well as over the long term. Perhaps as the theoretical and practical literature on the clinical use of Lacanian theory continues to grow, quantitative researchers will be able to isolate a set of particular therapeutic factors that are part and parcel of "Lacanian" therapy, and attempt to trace their impact in the long and short term as well. In fact, I can see a case to be made that certain techniques such as punctuation could at least become operationalized to the point of being able to be identified with some reliability by raters. Whatever happens in this regard, I am cautiously optimistic that, as psychological research continues to investigate the efficacy of treatments, it will also continue to reexamine the constraints it has placed upon what constitutes admissible evidence, strengthening quantitative research by increasing its external validity.

I should note also that this book focused largely upon subtle interventions, and brief statements or cues made by the therapist to encourage the patient's discourse to focus in a particular area. There were many moments in these therapies, however, when I was more verbal with these patients, but which were also aimed at following the letter of the patient's speech. Hence there may be a call for more case studies or brief illustrations of Lacanian therapy at moments when the clinician is more verbal with the patient.

Further, as I noted above, these case studies are lacking the patients' direct input. While patients and therapists often have vastly different impressions of what was helpful in the therapeutic process, and there is much debate to be had over why this is, that does not mean that we should shy away from exploring the similarities and differences in these assessments. Surely, an approach to therapy that has as its central aim the encouragement of the patient to speak, to say everything, might benefit by hearing more from its patients. While this may pose theoretical and clinical problems, it may still be valuable to the field to bring the rich content of the patient's speech into dialogue with the theoretical outlook of his therapist in a multiperspectival exploration of the nature of the Lacanian therapeutic interaction. This approach may take as its model research done by Walsh (2004) and others, which has attempted to utilize the perspectives of clinicians and patients to explore the question of what makes for good psychotherapy.

Finally—lest we forget that I am writing from an American perspective—there is the question of the seemingly ubiquitous time-limited psychotherapies. Even some of the most psychodynamically and psychoanalytically oriented clinics—many university counseling centers, for example—are currently seeing severe session limits as the only way to meet a burgeoning demand for therapy that quickly outpaces the availability of clinicians. Other clinics, such as community mental health centers, which have been traditionally psychodynamic and psychoanalytic, have been forced to the same measures because of the lack of reimbursement by insurance companies for more than 15 sessions. While this is a distasteful reality in many ways, there is also something good in our efforts to serve the greatest number, and why not make Lacanian technique available as part of our repertoire to those who do not have the means to pay clinicians out-of-pocket for indefinite periods of time? Lacan himself reminded us that the unconscious knows no time, and made unabashed use of this notion in his clinical work; there is no reason to believe that we cannot make use of his work in time-limited settings. The therapies described in this book were all relatively brief (2 years or less), but many clinics, such as university counseling centers, are limiting sessions to 15, 10, or even 5. Research may be called for that explores the possibility of using Lacanian theory in brief therapies.

THE WRITING PROCESS AND ITS LIMITS

The method used in this book—the clinical case study from the clinician's perspective—was limited in a number of ways. Issues of my subjectivity, the lack of alternative analyses of data, the incompleteness of the case presentations, and the absence in the final document of my original data all present limits to this work.

Like most clinical case studies, these were, in the end, a product of my own perspective, although I have by now presented these cases to other clinicians and theoreticians who have provided their critique and commentary. I have the blessing and the curse of having the final word on what I saw to be the motor forces in these therapies, at least within the confines of this document.

On a related note, I repeatedly encountered the inevitable frustration that must accompany any honest attempt to talk about clinical cases: the fact that I cannot tell the whole story. I have deeply disguised the case studies here, leaving major portions of the true stories out, and dramatically changing others. But even if there were no restrictions born of therapist–patient confidentiality, even if I could write forever, I would never be able to say everything. Setting out to write these cases, I naively hoped that I could at least give the reader the sense of an entire course of therapy for each patient, and follow the letter of some of the patient's speech as I did so, thus at least roughly reconstructing the therapies that I experienced. This hope was dashed early and often, however, as I realized that to follow even one small chain of signification in a patient's speech could have easily been the subject of an entire book, or even a life's work. Such is the nature of language, the inexhaustible Other.

Of course, psychotherapy is not made of discrete signifying chains that can be easily extricated from one another, and so when I have isolated them here, I have left more out than I would like. It would be impossible to re-create the kind of tracking of signifiers that occurred in psychotherapy here without embarking on a lifelong project.

Further, there is of course more to psychotherapy than language (indeed, there is more even to Lacanian theory than language), even if that has been our focus here. There are all the other moments that come together in a uniquely human endeavor—moments made up of an unlimited number of thoughts, associations, and affects, to put it in dry, psychological terms—which are left out here. I have been powerfully reminded many times of the impossibility of the psychoanalytic directive to "say everything" during the process of writing this book. When we take into account the dictates of strict confidentiality and clarity and concision of writing, we must resign ourselves to lose any pretension to completeness.

As a means of addressing this limitation, I read and reread the data that each study is based on throughout the writing process. Upon rereading the data, I looked to find alternate interpretations to those that I had presented in the case studies themselves. I also reread the data with an attunement to what I had left out of the case studies, and questioned why I had done so. The results of this exercise were numerous. I found a number of alternate readings of the data I had used, and ways to employ the data that I had not directly referenced to bolster those new interpretations. On the other hand, and in fact quite frequently, data that was left out of the final manuscript was supportive of the interpretations I have presented here, but it had to be struck for the sake of confidentiality and reasonable brevity.

What is left in this work, then, is a small sampling of decontextualized aspects of several courses of psychotherapy—a few brief glimpses of people in therapy—which hopefully stay true enough to their subjects while also conveying enough information about esoteric clinical phenomena to be useful to the reading clinician. While it was surprising and somewhat disappointing to run up against these limitations, it also renewed my awe for the tremendous complexity of the craft of psychotherapy, and of the ultimately ineffable aspects of human "psychology."

WHERE I FIT IN

I don't doubt that readers will notice that, despite my occasional comments about countertransference and my idiosyncratic reactions to theoretical and philosophical issues, I have not disclosed much that is personal here. There are a number of reasons for this, including my desire not to use the discussion of these patients in the context of an airing of my own personality and history. Moreover, in this book, I have tried to give priority to a careful exploration of theory and connection between it and clinical formulation and intervention. I may be accused of "intellectualizing" here, but that is really just what I mean to do.

That said, my relationship to this writing, as is perhaps that of any writer to his book, is complex, overdetermined, emotionally laden, and highly ambivalent to begin with. Yet it is complicated even more by the dual role that I played in this research: that of practitioner as well as researcher.

At the time that I saw these patients, I was not seeing them as sources of formal research data, and therefore my primary aims were simply to be the best clinician I could be for them, and of course, to learn from them. I was, however, engaged in a kind of experiment. As part of a larger process of trying to find a therapeutic and theoretical modality that best fit me and my patients, I was trying to use Lacanian theory in the psychotherapy setting.

I began my graduate training with very little sympathy for psychoanalytic thinking. Working with families after earning my master's degree, however, I began noticing, despite myself, some very psychoanalytic themes with my patients. I was a committed existentialist, but was quickly coming to realize that there were limitations to that vocabulary (just as there are to psychoanalysis, to be sure). One day, I was quite alarmed to hear myself quoting Freud in a discussion with my co-therapist on a family therapy case.

As time went on, I became strongly attracted to the writings of Freud and Lacan, thanks in no small part to the instruction of Dr. Bruce Fink. As my interest continued to grow, I became Dr.

Fink's supervisee, and therefore a great deal of my understanding of how Lacan can be translated into practice comes from his clinical supervision. Yet the therapeutic philosophy and methods I began to learn stood at odds with much of what I had learned before, which was influenced by more widely read psychodynamic theory, gestalt therapy, existential psychology, and "two-person" approaches, among others. This put me in a dilemma as a clinician, since I had very much enjoyed my experience using these models, yet it seemed that to put Lacan into practice, I had to radically shift my way of thinking and working with patients.

As years have gone by, I have struggled to make sense of what it means to use Lacan in a psychotherapeutic context. This directly maps onto the methodology of this book, which made use of the resultant copious notes I took on the language of my patients and my own interventions during our sessions.

One complication that arises from this dual role of clinician and writer/researcher is the fact that my own competence as a clinician is implicated in these chapters. I have tried to be aware, therefore, of the possibility that I could present myself as having been more clinically capable than I in fact was, or as having a better understanding of my patients than I in fact did. I don't imagine that I can entirely safeguard against this kind of problem, especially given the fact that these cases are heavily selective in what they present for the sake of clarity and confidentiality, and I cannot account for every motive, conscious and unconscious, for what I have left in and left out. Yet I have made a great deal of conscious effort not to aggrandize myself in my presentations of these treatments. For example, I have not placed anything in these cases about my behavior or clinical thinking that was not confirmed in my notes. I also decided to focus more on the process of therapy itself than on discussion of therapeutic outcomes in these case studies as a way of ensuring that this project did not become too much a function of my own desire to appear as a good clinician.

As I have written this book, it has had the potential of becoming a sort of continuation of the therapies, in which I could rewrite mistakes, create happier endings, and simplify messy, complicated sets of facts for their sakes as well as mine. As I said above, I imagine this is to some extent inevitable, but on the other hand, my connections with and respect for these four people have encouraged me throughout the process to be as careful as possible with the facts. I also tried not to make interpretations in the writing of these case studies that Caroline, Eric, Steve, and Jim had not at some point arrived at themselves.

As I am connected to these four people, I am also connected to the theory being presented here, and perhaps a word on my investment in it is appropriate. While I was indeed engaged in an experiment during these therapies, I would never have bothered if I did not find something attractive about the theory already. That being the case, I have at times found that being a psychotherapist who works with Lacanian theory can be a lonely prospect. I have alluded to this several times already, and indeed this fact is part of the impetus for having written this work. The marginal status of this theory—indeed, it lies at the margin of an already marginalized psychodynamic theory—can be a bit discouraging at times for a practitioner who decides to align himself with it but would still like to be able to have clinical conversations with his many colleagues.

In that spirit, I have made several comments that defend my thinking against the imagined objections of the reader throughout the text. In doing so, I am responding to reactions I have heard in actual conversations with other clinicians. Since I am writing with clinicians in mind, I feel it is helpful to address some of their likely questions and objections.

A LAST WORD

We psychologists have hardly been in a position to make an honest assessment of Lacan's potential contribution to psychotherapy. This is because (with very few exceptions) Lacan is not taught to psychology students, graduate or undergraduate, in the United

States. Not even in psychodynamic programs. My friends with philosophy degrees know him. My colleagues, for the most part, do not.

This need not be the case. I would hope that, given the many voices in the American psychoanalytic chorus, there is the chance to listen more closely to Lacan's. I can't say for certain that I have done Lacan any favors in this book (I suppose that depends in part on how willing the reader is to spell things backwards). Yet, for my part, I think his work is not just fodder for the academic exercises of Lacanian analysts, philosophers, and literature scholars. I suggest that it can be applied to real-life psychotherapies with real-life people. I invite you to judge for yourself; you've just read about four of them.

References

Alexander, F., & French, T. E. (1980). *Psychoanalytic therapy: Principles and application*. Lincoln, NE: University of Nebraska Press.

American Psychiatric Association. (2000). *Diagnostic and statistical manual of mental disorders* (4th edition, text revision). Washington, DC: American Psychiatric Association.

Balint, M. (1968). *The basic fault*. London: Tavistock.

Barkham, M., Margison, F., Leach, C., Lucock, M., Mellor, C.J., Evans, C., … McGrath, G. (2001). Service profiling and outcomes benchmarking using the CORE-OM: Toward practice-based evidence in the psychological therapies. *Journal of Consulting and Clinical Psychology*, 69, 184–196.

Bergin, A. E. (1997). Neglect of the therapist and the human dimensions of change: A commentary. *Clinical Psychology: Science and Practice*, *4*, 83–89.

Beutler, L. E. (1997). The psychotherapist as a neglected variable in psychotherapy: An illustration by reference to the role of therapist experience and training. *Clinical Psychology: Science and Practice*, *4*, 44–52.

Bickman, L. (1999). Practice makes perfect and other myths about mental health services. *American Psychologist*, *54*, 965–978.

Bohart, A. C. (2000). Paradigm clash: Empirically supported treatments versus empirically supported psychotherapy practice. *Psychotherapy Research*, *10*, 488–493.

Bohart, A., O'Hara, M., & Leitner, L. (1998). Empirically violated treatments: Disenfranchisement of humanistic and other psychotherapies. *Psychotherapy Research, 8*(2), 141–157.

Butler, J. (1993). *Bodies that matter: On the discursive limits of sex.* New York: Routledge.

Davanloo, H. (1990). *Unlocking the unconscious: Selected papers of Habib Davanloo, M. D.* Chichester, UK: Wiley.

Davies, J. M. (2004). Whose bad objects are we anyway? Repetition and our elusive love affair with evil. *Psychoanalytic Dialogues, 14*(6), 711–732.

Dor, J., Gurewich, J. F., & Fairfield, S. (1997a). *Introduction to the reading of Lacan: The unconscious structured like a language.* Northvale, NJ: Jason Aronson.

Dor, J., Gurewich, J. F., & Fairfield, S. (1997b). *The clinical Lacan.* Northvale, NJ: Jason Aronson.

Ensler, E. (2001). *The vagina monologues.* New York: Random House.

Feldstein, R., Fink, B., & Jaanus, M. (1996). *Reading seminars I and II.* Albany, NY: State University of New York Press.

Felman, S. (1988). On reading poetry: Reflections on the limits and possibilities of psychoanalytic approaches. In J. Muller & W. Richardson (Eds.), *The purloined Poe: Lacan, Derrida, and psychoanalytic reading* (pp.). Baltimore, MD: Johns Hopkins University Press.

Fink, B. (1995). *The Lacanian subject: Between language and jouissance.* Princeton, NJ: Princeton University Press.

Fink, B. (1997). *A clinical introduction to Lacanian psychoanalysis: Theory and technique.* Cambridge, MA: Harvard University Press.

Fink, B. (2003). The use of Lacanian psychoanalysis in a case of fetishism. *Clinical Case Studies, 2*(1), 50–69.

Fink, B. (2004). *Lacan to the letter: Reading Écrits closely.* Minneapolis, MN: University of Minnesota Press.

Fink, B. (2007). *Fundamentals of psychoanalytic technique: A Lacanian approach for practitioners.* New York: W.W. Norton and Company.

Frankel, L. (2003). Hands off! The taboo surrounding males' first ejaculation. In Heasly R. and Crane, B., (Eds.) *Sexual lives: A reader on the theories and realities of human sexualities* (pp. 307–317). New York: McGraw-Hill.

Freud, S. (1900). The interpretation of dreams. In J. Strachey (Ed. & Trans.), *The standard edition of the complete psychological works of Sigmund Freud* (Vol. 4 & 5). London: Hogarth Press.

Freud, S. (1904). The psychopathology of everyday life. In J. Strachey (Ed. & Trans.), *The standard edition of the complete psychological works of Sigmund Freud* (Vol. 6). London: Hogarth Press.

Freud, S. (1905a). Fragments of an analysis of a case of hysteria. In J. Strachey (Ed. & Trans.), *The standard edition of the complete psychological works of Sigmund Freud* (Vol. 7, pp. 1–122). London: Hogarth Press.

Freud, S. (1905b). Jokes and their relation to the unconscious. In J. Strachey (Ed. & Trans.), *The standard edition of the complete psychological works of Sigmund Freud* (Vol. 8). London: Hogarth Press.

Freud, S. (1909). Notes upon a case of obsessional neurosis. In J. Strachey (Ed. & Trans.), *The standard edition of the complete psychological works of Sigmund Freud* (Vol. 10, pp. 153–249). London: Hogarth Press.

Freud, S. (1916). Introductory lectures on psycho-analysis. In J. Strachey (Ed. & Trans.), *The standard edition of the complete psychological works of Sigmund Freud* (Vol. 15 & 16). London: Hogarth Press.

Freud, S. (1918). The taboo of virginity (Contributions to the psychology of love III). *The standard edition of the complete psychological works of Sigmund Freud* (Volume 11, pp. 191–208). London: Hogarth Press.

Freud, S., & Breuer, J. (1895). Studies on hysteria. In J. Strachey (Ed. & Trans.), *The standard edition of the complete psychological works of Sigmund Freud* (Vol. 2). London: Hogarth Press.

Gallop, J. (1985). *Reading Lacan*. Ithaca, NY: Cornell University Press.

Godfried, M. R., & Wolfe, B. E. (1996). Psychotherapy practice and research: Repairing a strained alliance. *American Psychologist, 51*, 1007–1016.

Goldman, Y. (2004). *Neurosis and fantasy: Lacanian theory and case conceptualization through three case studies*. Doctoral Dissertation, Duquesne University, Pittsburgh, PA.

Heidegger, M. (1927/1962). *Being and time* (J. Macquarrie & E. Robinson, Trans.). New York: Harper and Row.

Jacobs, T. J. (1991). *The use of the self: Countertransference and communication in the analytic situation*. Madison, CT: International Universities Press.

Kahane, C., & Bernheimer, C. (1990). *In Dora's case: Freud—hysteria—feminism*. New York: Columbia University Press.

Lacan, J. (1988a). *The seminar of Jacques Lacan, book I: Freud's papers on technique, 1953–1954* (J. A. Miller, Ed., J. Forester, Trans). New York: W. W. Norton.

Lacan, J. (1988b). *The seminar of Jacques Lacan, book II: The ego in Freud's theory and in the technique of psychoanalysis, 1954–1955* (J. A. Miller, Ed., S. Tomaselli, Trans.). New York: W. W. Norton.

Lacan, J. (1994). *Le séminaire livre IV: La relation d'objet, 1956–1957* (J.-A. Miller, Ed.). Paris: Seuil.

Lacan, J. (1998). *The seminar of Jacques Lacan, book XX, encore: On feminine sexuality, the limits of love and knowledge, 1972–1973* (B. Fink, Trans.). New York: W. W. Norton. (Original published in 1975).

Lacan, J. (2002). Aggressiveness in psychoanalysis. In *Écrits: A selection* (B. Fink, Trans.) (pp. 10–30). New York: W. W. Norton. (Original work published in 1948).

Lacan, J. (2002). The mirror stage as formative of the I function as revealed in psychoanalytic experience. In *Écrits: A selection* (B. Fink, Trans.) (pp. 3–9). New York: W. W. Norton. (Original published in 1949).

Lacan, J. (2002). The function and field of speech and language in psychoanalysis. In *Écrits: A selection* (B. Fink, Trans.) (pp. 31–106). New York: W. W. Norton. (Original published in 1953).

Lacan, J. (2002). The instance of the letter in the unconscious, or reason since Freud. In *Écrits: A selection* (B. Fink, Trans.) (pp. 138–168). New York: W. W. Norton. (Original published in 1957).

Lacan, J. (2002). The signification of the phallus. In *Écrits: A selection* (B. Fink, Trans.) (pp. 271–280). New York: W. W. Norton. (Original published in 1958).

Lacan, J. (2002). The subversion of the subject and the dialectic of desire in the Freudian unconscious. In *Écrits: A selection* (B. Fink, Trans.) (pp. 281–312). New York: W. W. Norton. (Original published in 1960).

Lacan, J. (2002). The direction of the treatment and the principles of its power. In *Écrits: A selection* (B. Fink, Trans.) (pp. 215–270). New York: W. W. Norton. (Original published in 1961).

Lacan, J. (2006). Presentation on the transference. In *Ecrits: The first complete edition in English* (B. Fink, Trans.) (pp. 176–188). New York: W. W. Norton. (Original published in 1951).

Lacan, J. (2006). Seminar on "The Purloined Letter." In *Écrits: The first complete edition in English* (B. Fink, Trans.) (pp. 6–50). New York: W. W. Norton. (Original published in 1966).

Lacan, J. (2006). *Écrits: The first complete edition in English*. New York: W. W. Norton.

Lacan, J., and Copjec J. (1990). Television: *A challenge to the psychoanalytic establishment*. New York: W.W. Norton and Company.

Leclaire, S. (1956). Jerome, or death in the life of the obsessional. In *Returning to Freud: Clinical psychoanalysis in the school of Lacan* (S. Schneiderman, Ed. & Trans.). New Haven, CT: Yale University Press, 1980.

Leclaire, S. (1958). Philo, or the obsessional and his desire. In *Returning to Freud: Clinical psychoanalysis in the school of Lacan* (S. Schneiderman, Ed. & Trans.). New Haven, CT: Yale University Press, 1980.

Leichsenring, F., & Rabung, S. (2008). Effectiveness of long term psychoanalytic and psychodynamic psychotherapy: A meta-analysis. *Journal of the American Medical Association, 300*, 1551–1565.

Lerner, H. (1988). *Women in therapy*. Northvale, NJ: Jason Aronson, 1991.

Malone, K. R., & Friedlander, S. R. (2000). *The subject of Lacan: A Lacanian reader for psychologists*. Albany, NY: State University of New York Press.

Maroda, K. J. (1999). *Seduction, surrender, and transformation: Emotional engagement in the analytic process*. Hillsdale, NJ: Analytic Press.

Maroda, K. J. (2001). *The power of countertransference: Innovations in analytic technique*. Chickchester, NY: Wiley.

McWilliams, N. (1994). *Psychoanalytic diagnosis: Understanding personality structure in the clinical process*. New York: Guilford Press.

Miller, A. (1997). *The drama of the gifted child* (R. Ward, Trans.). New York: Basic Books.

Nobus, D. (2000). *Jacques Lacan and the Freudian practice of psychoanalysis*. London: Routledge.

O'Donnell, J. M. (1979). The crisis of experimentalism in the 1920s: E. G. Boring and his uses of history. *American Psychologist, 34*, 289–295.

Poe, E. A. (1912). The purloined letter. In *Tales of mystery and imagination*. London: J. M. Dent & Sons. (Original published in 1845).

Rabate, J. (2000). *Lacan in America*. New York: Other Press.

Renik, O. (1999). Playing one's cards face up in psychoanalysis: An approach to the problem of self disclosure. *Psychoanalytic Quarterly, 68*, 521–539.

Roazen, P. (1995). *How Freud worked: First-hand accounts of patients*. Northvale, NJ: Jason Aronson.

Rogers, C. (1995). *On becoming a person: A therapist's view of psychotherapy*. New York: Houghton Mifflin.

Rosenthal, R. (1966). *Experimenter effects in behavioral research*. New York: Appleton.

Roustang, F. (1990). *The Lacanian delusion*. New York: Oxford University Press.

Saussure, S. (1986). *Course in general linguistics* (A. Riedlinger, A. Sechehaye, & C. Bally, Eds., R. Harris, Trans.). LaSalle, IL: Open Court.

Schaetzel, J. C. (1973). Bronzehelmet, or the itinerary of the psychotherapy of a psychotic. In S. Schneiderman (Ed. & Trans.), *Returning to Freud: Clinical psychoanalysis in the school of Lacan*. New Haven, CT: Yale University Press, 1980.

Schneiderman, S. (Ed. & Trans.). (1980). *Returning to Freud: Clinical psychoanalysis in the school of Lacan*. New Haven, CT: Yale University Press.

Schneiderman, S. (1983). *Jacques Lacan: The death of an intellectual hero*. Cambridge, MA: Harvard University Press.

Shedler, J. (2010). The efficacy of psychodynamic psychotherapy. *American Psychologist*, *65*(2), 98–109.

Soler, C. (1996). Hysteria and obsession. In R. Feldstein & B. Fink (Eds.), *Reading seminars I and II*. Albany, NY: State University of New York Press.

Spinelli, E. (1997). *Tales of un-knowing: Eight stories of existential therapy*. New York: New York University Press.

Tostain, R. (1968). Fetishization of a phobic object. In S. Schneiderman (Ed.), *Returning to Freud: Clinical psychoanalysis in the school of Lacan*. New Haven, CT: Yale University Press, 1980.

Walsh, R. (2004). What is good psychotherapy? *Journal of Humanistic Psychology*, *20*(10), 1–13.

Winnicott, D. (1971). *Playing and reality*. London: Tavistock.

Winnicott, D. (1986). *Holding and interpretation: Fragment of an analysis*. New York: Grove Press.

Yin, R. (1989). *Case study research: Design and method*. London: Sage Publications.

Index

G

H

I

M

V

W